W9-BUE-624

A HISTORY OF THE FUTURE

A Study of the Four Major Eschatologies

Christopher C. Hong

UNIVERSITY
PRESS OF
AMERICA

To John Hamilton Skilton
Professor of New Testament Emeritus
Westminster Theological Seminary
My first and best teacher of
New Testament Greek and
Textual Criticism

iii

CONTENTS

PREFACE

In the study of world religions, one can readily discover religious stratification into at least three main layers: animistic-dynamic, noetic-psychic, and fideo-pneumatic. One thing that cuts vertically through all these strata is a common belief in a power well denoted by the Polynesian word <u>mana</u>. The word <u>mana</u> simply means an extraphysical power immanent in and emanating from nature, viewed as the embodiment of all the elemental forces that produce and maintain the order of the universe. Although these three religious strata exist in almost every religion except the Judeo-Christian, one particular stratum is predominant in religious sentience.

Among the ancient Babylonians and Egyptians, and also among the Shintoists, animistic-dynamism dominated their religious consciousness. For them experience and chance were the most important sources of knowledge of the things of nature. The noetic-psychic religious consciousness worked primarily on cognitive reasoning or inference, and was oriented toward the discovery of the real self; on this level man himself became an arbiter of his own destiny. This was the case, for example, with the Greek Olympians, the Hindus, and the Buddhists. The fideo-pneumatic religious consciousness was, in a sense, the divine consciousness which was implanted objectively from the wholly other world. A spirit from the objective realm controlled the religious sentience. Zoroastrianism is one good example from this layer. Judaism and Christianity also belong to this religious layer; however, in clear distinction from the others, they totally lacked the progression and evolution from the

vii

animistic-dynamic through the noetic-psychic
to the fideo-pneumatic religious
consciousness. In the Biblical account (Gen.
1-11), men at the beginning of history were
monotheistic, but their religion gradually
degenerated into fetishistic, animistic, and
pantheistic polytheism. However, Judasim and
Christianity maintained the original
monotheism, the centrum of which is a fideo-
pneumaic religious belief.

In the development of the various forms
of religion with a single predominant religious consciousness, there have been four
different forms of eschatology: the
historic-terminal, the circular, the
supernal, and the historic-linear. The
English word "eschatology" is derived from
the Greek <u>eschatos</u>, meaning "the last thing."
Simply expressed, eschatology is the teaching
of the last things. It can be viewed from
two main perspectives; in one respect, it
relates to the fate of individuals after
death. This involves a number of issues such
as the survival of individual personality,
the immortality of the soul, the resurrection
of the body, and the final judgment. In the
other respect, it relates to certain
cataclysmic events that bring about the
destruction or renewal of the present world,
to heaven and hell, and to eternal state.

In the present study, a few out of many
different religions have been singled out to
establish the four distinctive systems of
eschatology. While the ancient Babylonians,
the Olympian Greeks, and the Shintoists
expressed an historic-terminal eschatology,
the Orphics and the Hindu-Buddhists favored a
circular eschatology. On the other hand,
while the ancient Egyptians and the Parsees
or Zoroastrians espoused a supernal
eschatology, the Jews and Christians held to

an historic-linear eschatology. The author
has made an earnest effort to define and
describe these four distinctive
eschatologies, and in so doing has incurred
an enormous debt to many scholars whose ideas
and thoughts have become so much a part of
himself that he is not quite sure which is
theirs and which is his own. He wishes to
acknowledge his indebtedness to many; their
works in part are acknowledged in footnotes.
The author also wishes to thank Mr. Robert
Lind, the assistant city editor of the Forum,
a Fargo, North Dakota newspaper, Dr. Arne
Teigland and Mr. Calvin Libby; they had
proofread the entire work. Many thanks
should be offered to Mrs. Darlene Gunderson,
whose assistance as an excellent typist has
been indispensible. Finally, the author owes
many thanks to his wife, Soonie, for her
invaluable support and help during the
writing of this work.

Moorhead, Minnesota

Chapter 1

The Historic-Terminal Eschatology

The Ancient Babylonians

A general attitude of the ancient
Babylonia appeared to be the unwillingness to
conceive of anything as being inanimate.
They had seen their world as being filled
with the animistic forces.[1] These forces
seemed to them, however, as not being con-
fined to physical bodies. In their daily
experience, these forces were capable of
moving about free of physical limitations,
and invisible to human eyes. Thus their phenomenal world was inhabited by the forces
which were thoroughly alive and active,
expressive, responsive, and capable of things
of their own volition.

This general attitude toward nature
appeared to be a sort of adjustment and in
conformity to new circumstances which the
Sumerians had created. The Sumerians looked
upon the cosmos ("world" or "universe") as a
partaker at once of the qualities of man,
nature, and a supernal being or a final
cause. What they confronted was not three
separate entities but rather one thing with
different aspects of the primary unity. They
thought of nature as an indwelling spirit and
a personal living being. For the modern
scientific man, the phenomenal world is primarily an "it" seen objectively, but for the
Sumero-Babylonians it was a "thou." In
their world view, the thing confronted by
them was unique, and it was known directly
and without the articulation. It was
experienced as a life confronting a life, and
the encounter between a thing in nature and
man always resulted in an "I-thou"
relationship.[2] The nature here was not
sharply set off as something different from

man. Rather, man and nature were bound
together in one moral order. The cosmos commanded a moral imperative, and when a man
acts toward a thing in nature, his action was
said to be dictated by moral consideration.

Under the long standing influence that
came from the Sumerian cultural antecedent,
the ancient Babylonians came to the awareness
that they were surrounded by the animistic
spirits. From the human point of view this
awareness was of great importance, because
these spirits were belived to excite their
interest in human life and destiny. These
forces might turn out to be either friends or
foes, and as such may determine the whole
course of human life. Therefore the
Babylonians' main concern was to cultivate
the good will of these spirits and to secure
their assistance.

For the sake of cultivating such good
will, the Babylonians had developed the
strange rites and ceremonies. In fact, the
primary aim of their cult as a whole was to
avert anger of these spirits, and by so doing
they hoped for securing their assistance in
the struggle for living. As anger is aroused
among men by improper conduct, so it was
believed to be with these spirits. One must
be careful to do the things which are
pleasing to them. Thus the essential part of
the Babylonian religion was not belief, but
practice. Their religion was seen as the
proper manner by which to approach the
spirits. Their cult was oriented toward the
establishment of good will between the
spirits and the votaries. The purpose of
their rites was to set into motion the animistic forces inherent in certain substances-
-the flesh of sacrifices, incense, oil,
water, wine, fire, and so on; in certain
forms--numbers, figures, pictures, and other
symbols; and in certain activities--gestures,
dance, procession, songs, and dramas.

The whole religious gravity in the Babylonian society had been on the side of practice and on mundane affairs. This is evident in an elaborate system of prohylaxis against the so-called "seven" spirits, whose potency derived from the primodial realm, and who were capable of working good. For protection against perils from the "seven" spirits, or for the deliverance in the event of being already attacked by them, the ancient Babylonians had the prophylaxis of rites and rituals in many forms, including the wearing of amulets.

The amulets were invented as a result of incidental experience. For example, against the apalling discomfort of the hot west wind that in summer brings sandstorms from the Arabian desert, they wore somthing. From this experience, an amulet, which means something to carry or wear against the invisible forces, was devised in different forms. Their amulets were of two kinds, those which were inscribed with all sorts of magic formulas and those which were not. Earlier the magic formulas were recited over the amulets which were worn by the living or placed on the dead. Later, the words of the magical formulas were inscribed on the amulets in order to bring about a double power, that is, the power that was supposed to be inherent in the material of which the amulet was made and the power which lay in the magic words inscribed on it.

When a victim already showed symptoms of demonic possession, a magician was called in to diagnose the malady and to expel the evil being. This was done by reciting the proper incantation with the appropriate ritual, often by invoking a god, most often Marduk, although not all the gods were equally potent in assisting suffering humanity. The priests concerned with deliverance from evil spirits were the exorcists who performed the

3

appropriate incantations and rituals, often
in association with the actual surgical or
medical techniques, and also with a symbolic
action to dispose of the evil curse.[3] They
are not only the exorcists in our term but
also the magicians.

Modern natural scientists generally
regard magic as an elaborate and systematic
pseudo-science, a suprious system of natural
law, and a fallacious guide of conduct.
Magic, however, in the Babylonian definition,
is an act of bringing about results beyond
human power by recourse to superhuman
spirit-agencies, Satan and demons.

Both personal and impersonal forms
of magics have been observed. The former is
little more than superstition when natural
law is thought to be set aside or influenced
by incantation, spells, amulets, charms,
etc., apart from the intervention of spiritual beings. With the latter, however, the
living, intelligent spiritual beings become
the real agents. By the use of incantations
and ceremonies, men actually influence and
even control these spirit-agents. The activity of such supernatural agents produces the
extraordinary phenomena that transcend the
normal operation of the physical law and our
sense perception.

Although the Babylonian magicians often
had claimed that their magical techniques
were revealed by their favorite deities, they
usually called upon the self-operating forces
which were belived to be independent of the
gods, who themselves also had to call upon
these forces for their own benefit. In fact,
the Babylonians portrayed their gods as the
most powerful magicians, and Marduk was the
greatest of all. In general, magic was practiced in a "pure" form that had no concern
with the divine will. Rather, it was viewed
as automatically effective, and even capable

of coercing the gods to do the will of the votaries.

Calamities and misfortunes could be avoided if one had some sort of foreknowledge about future events. The Babylonians had really believed that the divine intentions were very often foreshadowed in the past historical events. This conviction was very strong among the Babylonians. In their view, what had taken place in one part of the world was mirrored in another part. Accordingly, they observed the earthly happenings--even the most trivial--with very inquisitive minds.

They often reasoned that if a certain event succeeded another in time, there existed a possible causual connection between them, and the same result might be expected to succeed the same event on another occasion. In accordance with this manner of viewing the things on earth, the lists of unusual occurences with the standard sequences were drawn up, and a great pseudo-science resulted. This pseudo-science eventually received a common designation, "divination," the term deriving from Latin divinare, "to foresee."

Divination is but a species of magic employed as a means of securing secret and illegitimate knowledge, especially of the future. A diviner professed to predict future events. Two distinct forms of divination in the ancient Babylonian society were known: artificial or augural divination and inspirational or intuitive divination. The former, which is also known today as inductive divination, interprets certain signs or omens. On the other hand, in the latter, the medium is completely under the influence of a demonic power, which enables him to foresee the future and utter oracles emobodying what

5

he saw. The diviners worked through some native super faculty.

Sometimes the Babylonians used a substitute in order to divert an evil attack. A wax image or the form of an animal was placed alongside the afflicted and identified with him in detail. The evil spirits were supposed to be transferred from the victim to the substitute through the ritual ceremony.

When the higher culture was introduced into the Babylonian city-states, some of these animistic forces, were soon conceived of as the gods, and the polytheisn had become their religion. Admittedly it is difficult for us to comprehend the causes of polytheism. Nevertheless, it appears that the Babylonians had speculated about the inner relationship among the city-state patron gods, and they placed these patron deities in a hierarchy along the line of their cosmology.[4] According to their cosmology, the universe was made up of an-ki, "heaven-earth." The earth was seen as a flat-disk, and heaven as a hollow space enclosed at the top and bottom by a solid surface in the shape of a vault. The space between heaven and earth was filled with a substance called lil, "wind" or "air." The most characteristic feature of lil was movement and expansion. Surrounding the an-ki there was the boundless sea, in which the cosmos somehow remained fixed and immovable. Then the basic components of the cosmos were heaven, earth, sea, and atmosphere. To these spheres the gods were stationed, and the most politically prominent city-states were able to put their gods into a triad of Anu, Enlil, and Enki (Ea).

Anu originally had the main seat of worship at Urek (Ereck) and was given the sphere of heaven. He was elevated to the heaven, or to the sky god (=Zeus=Jupiter). At

one time he was regarded by the Sumerians as
the supreme ruler of the pantheon. Anu continued to be worshiped in Sumer throughout
the millenniums, but he lost much of his
prominence to Enlil. Enlil, from the time of
the earliest intelligible records, was known
as "the father of the gods" and "the king of
all the lands." The god Enlil is the one who
was supposed to have given the Babylonian
kings the kingship of the land and the
sceptor. He was generally regarded as a
beneficient deity who was responsible for the
planning and creating of most productive
features of the cosmos. He was said to
establish plenty, abundance, and prosperity
in the land. The god Enki or Ea was the god
of wisdom and magic, who organized the earth
as the "lord of ki" ("subterranean region"),
in accordance with the decision of Enlil, who
made only the general plans. The actual
detials and execution were left to Enki.

Along with these triad deities, the most
popular deities were the goddess Innini at
Urek and her male consort, Tammuz. The
Semitics later identified Innini with Ishtar,
whose fame and worship spread in Syria and
Palestine. She appeared in Syria in the name
of Astarte and in the Old Testament she was
recorded as Ashtaroth. Ishtar, which was her
most common name, was goddess of war and love
and of procreation; she was a fertility
goddess. A distinction was made between the
earthly Ishtar and the heavenly Ishtar. The
former represented reproduction, and the
latter stood literally and figuratively for
the heavenly brightness and light, and was an
idealized mother to the whole human race.
Her male partner, Tammuz, was variously
reported to be her son, her brother, or her
lover. His other name, Damu-zi in the old
Sumerian form, "faithful son," indicates that
at first he was considered the son of the
Mother Earth. He was associated with grain
and flowers, and was called "Good Shepherd."

At a very early date, Tammuz and Ishtar were worshipped in Syria, especially at Byblos. At the turning of the seventh century B.C. they were worshiped in Palestine and reached Egypt, where the cult assimilated into the Osiris-Isis worship. In Greece, the Tammuz-Ishtar cult appeared in the form of the myth of Demeter and Persephone. There Ishtar also was identified with Aphrodite. In Enuma Elish, a new supreme god Marduk played the main character in the theogony and in the struggle between the two parties of Tiama and Ea-Marduk over supremacy.

The Sumero-Babylonian gods were not conceived as absolute supernatural beings. The Babylonians believed that there existed a realm of the supernal above their gods, whose decrees the gods must obey. Their gods were said to belong to, and to be created from, this primordial realm. Their gods were not the source of all that are, nor did they transcend the universe. They are rather part of the realm precedent to and independent of them. They were bound by and subservient to the laws of the primordial realm. Some of their gods were regarded as the creators and sustainers of the world of man, but transcending them were the primordial autonomous forces. Thus their gods were mythical. In myth the gods appear not only as actors, but also as acted upon. At the heart of the Babylonian myth there is a tension between gods and the primordial forces which shaped their god's destinies.[5] In truth, a myth describes the unfolding destiny of gods, giving expression to the idea that, beside the will of the gods, there are other, independent forces which wholly or in part determine all destinies.

The ancient Babylonians, nevertheless, daily approached their gods with fear and reverence. Their gods were supposed to punish the evil-doers and reward the just.

But it was only the present life which was
thought to be affected by the reward and
punishment. Beyond the grave there was no
retribution. Therefore, for instance, their
prayers were made not for a happy eternal
life or for help to avoid the divine wrath in
the world to come. They almost exclusively
offered the prayers for temporal benefit, for
a long life on earth, prosperity, victory
over enemies, and the like.

A general feeling about the future life
was pesimistic and negative. They had taken
very negative attitudes toward their future
with a common share that beyond the grave
there was nothing waiting worthy of living.
In earlier times, the dead seemed to have
been thought of as continuing membership in
his own family, because the dead were usually
buried under the house in which the remaining
members of the family lived. Later, however,
a new thought was added to this. In some
mysterious way the dead from his grave took a
journey toward a ghostly town of seven walls
beneath the earth. The real final destiny of
the dead now was the dark domain of
Ereshkigal, "queen of the underworld,"
inside the earth, where all the dead were
received, and from which none were allowed to
depart.

The kur, "mountain," another term for this
final abode of the dead, corresponds to the
Greek Hades and to the Hebrew Sheol. The
kur, cosmologically speaking, implies the
empty space between the earth crust and the
primeval sea. The Babylonians used to think
of the earth as one great mountain, and deep
down inside this great mountain was the abode
of the dead.[6] Sometimes this place was called
aralu, a name of uncertain etymology. In the
story of the "Descent of Ishtar," the way to
aralu is barred by a gate bolted and guarded
by a porter. Beyond this gate there are six
other gates, through which Ishtar had to pass

before finding herself in the presence of the goddess Allatu. Allatu appeared to have supreme authority over the realm of the dead.[7]

The Babylonians did not entertain the idea of resurrection in any form. Once a man had been carried off to Aralu, no one, even gods, could bring him back. Therefore they designated the underworld "the land without return." The dead were not, however, necessarily imprisoned in Aralu. The dead could return under certain conditions to plague the living. There were rites and incantations to be employed in case a man had been seized or taken possession of by a spirit (utukku, "ghost") from the dead. In such cases there is no question of resurrection but only of the spirit returning to the earth for a shorter or longer period. When the goddess Ishtar was to be released from Aralu, Namtar, at the command of Allatu, sprinkled her with "the waters of life." The Babylonian word for "to live" has also the meaning of "to receive health." Now Ishtar, on arriving before Allatu, had been struck with diverse maladies. The sprinkling with "the water of life" simply was to restore her health of body and fit her for return to the company of the gods.

There are texts which appear to attribute to the gods the power of restoring life in the literal sense. Marduk is called "the merciful who loves to restore the dead to life." Gula, the goddess of healing, is "she who gives life to the dead." But these expressions are the metaphors and epithets which appear chiefly in incantations and hymns addressed to the gods for some specific purpose, such as delivering a victim from disease.

The Babylonians had given a special honor to every god and in particular to Marduk and

Ninib for their work of the revivification of
nature. The rerurn of vegetation in spring
was hailed as the work of Marduk, and Ninib
was said to have filled what appeared to be
dead with new life.[7] Similarly, their gods
could restore the suffering individuals stri-
ken with disease to new life. It is this
"restoration" which lies in the power of the
gods, but once a man had been carried off to
Aralu, even the gods cannot bring him back to
this earth.

In the Epic of Gilgasmesh[8], Gilgamesh in
anguish invoked the shade of his friend
Enkidu. Enkidu's utukku ("ghost") came forth
from a hole in the ground "like a wind" and
was at once recognized by this friend. But
Gilgamesh was informed once more of the inevitability of death and the sad state of
those who had passed into Aralu.

The myth of Adapa[9] conveys the same idea
that a man has no hope for the future. Adapa
was the son of Ea, the god of wisdom. He was
priest-king of Eridu, the oldest of the
Babylonian cities. Ea had created him "as
the model of man," and had given him wisdom,
but not eternal life. His priestly duties
were to provide the table of the gods with
fish. One day he was fishing when the south
wind blew and overturned his boat. In rage
he broke the wings of the south wind, and
thus there was no wind for seven days.
Illabrat, the messenger of Anu, was sent to
inquire as to the reason for it. Adapa was
summoned before Anu. Ea stood by Adapa,
advising him what course to take for his own
safety. Adapa was to go with his hair
uncombed and dressed as a mourner. The
guards of the gate would ask him why he was
in mourning. Adapa was to reply, "two gods
have disappeared from our land, for that
reason I am thus." The guards would ask,
"who are the two gods?" Adapa was to answer
"Tammuz and Ningizzida."

11

These were in fact the two guards
themselves, and the advice was to gain for
Adapa favorable introduction to Anu. Ea also
warned that Adapa would be offered bread and
water of death, and he was not to eat or
drink. When Adapa made the journey Tammuz
and Ningizzida spoke to Anu on his behalf and
secured the favorable admission to Anu. Anu
was appeased, and offered to Adapa the bread
of life, but Adapa, recalling Ea's advice,
refused to eat of it. So Adapa lost his
chance of obtaining immortality and was sent
back to earth.

Both the Epic of Gilgamesh
and the story of Adapa had shown the general
feeling among the ancient Babylonians about
their future life. The general feeling had
been that man had no right to eternal life
and that their gods zealously guarded the
secret of immortality off from mankind. It
was only by an exceptional chance and acci-
dent that Gilgamesh's relative, Utnapishtim,
should have acquired the blessing of
immortality. Gilgamesh himself almost succeeded in obtaining immortality, but returned
home with empty hands after a long journey to
search for the secret of immortality. He,
too, had to face the common fate that eventually had carried him away into Aralu, a
dusty place of no-return. The dead hero
Gilgamesh, however, had the special privilege
of becoming "the judge of the underworld."

The Olympian Greeks

Here the Olympian Greeks are meant the
ancient Greeks who addressed themselves to
the twelve Olympian gods.[10] Their attitude
toward their future life hereafter also was a
sort of complete pessimism. Old age was
thought of as a grievous evil, no less than
death. In their eyes death was, however, not
extinction, but the separation of an indivi-

dual psyche from the body. The body was the
only source of joy in life. Death meant an
existence deprived of all that made life
worth living. It was meant for all alike,
with few exceptions, who would pass into a
mere shadow of existence, in which the psyche
or the soul could do no more than engage in a
kind of pale reflection of its earthly
activities. The departed were said to live
both in their graves and in a land of the
dead, governed by Hades.

A few , however, were exempted from this
gloomy life after death. These were the
"heros," men of good family.[11] The average
Greeks believed that anyone powerful or
otherwise remarkable in life continued to be
so even after death. From this belief, the
hero cult sprang. When a hero died, he
became daimon, the possessor of mana. Daimon
signifies a superhuman being of somthing less
than a divine rank. Its proper abode was
nether heaven, in between heaven and earth,
where the aer filled in. Corresponding to
this intermediate sphere, the daimons were
superior to men on earth and inferior to the
gods in heaven.

In search for the origin of the daimon-
hero cult, we recognize that the idea of the
daimons represents man's religious experience
with the animistic forces in nature. The
ordinary Greeks felt that they were living
under the influence of some sort of "power"
(daimonios), of something wonderful, incomprehensible, and irrational. They had often experienced "powers," but they were unable to
explain their experience and these supernatural powers. Their experience with "powers"
was gradually changed into a belief in "the
powers" which may be good or bad, and subject
to passions, as men are, and therefore capable
of doing unreasonable things, of departing
from strict justice to serve some personal
end, of being angry or amorous, and so on.

The daimons of the heros were believed to walk invisibly on earth, guarding mankind and bringing prosperity to them. The hero-daimons had, however, some limitations in their power. Their power was said to have been bound up with their physical remains. The hero-daimons were not able to do anything good or ill far from their graves and from the places where their bones lay. Hence there was on occasion keen competition for the possession of these relics. The Athenians brought back from the island of Skyros some bones supposed to be those of Theseus. Sparta recovered from Tegen certain reamins identified with those of Otistes. Thebes boasted the possession of Hektor's body, fetched from Troy in obedience to an oracle. Hence a city-state might have founded a hero-cult either in expectation of benefits to come, or to avert the effects of the dead man's wrath. This belief was so firm that if a city suffered from a plague or other disasters, it was often thought that the cause must be neglect of a great man's spirit, and the oracle was consulted to find out who it was.

Although none of the Olympian Greeks had any wish to go to the underworld, a gloomy and shadowy place, there was no yearning among them for immortality. Their only interest was joy and happiness in present life, in which also the Olympian gods had vested interest. Their pessimism and negativism toward future life and their sole mundane interest and concern seem to have been a by-product of their view of the Olympian gods themselves, that is to say, the by-product of the cognizance of the Olympian gods' "being" and the domain or the sphere of action.[12]

The cognizance of the divine being has to do with two things, namely, the sphere and the identity of the divine beings. The sphere of the Olympians consisted of the material or phenomenal world, which we can perceive with our sense organs, and the spiritual or numenal world, which can only be grasped by the mind, being quite imperceptable to any sense. Later, a different opinion about the numenal world emerged. According to the Platonists, for instance, the numenal world is immaterial, but, according to the Stoics, it consists of very rare and fine "matter," while the coarser elements constitute the greater part of the world we live in.

The sphere in which the Olympian gods dwelt is all above and beyond the phenomenal world and was also called "heaven." The Greek word for "heaven" is not, however, ouranos but aither. It was in the aither that the gods lived, and aither itself was divine. Beneath or below the sphere of aither there was another sphere which was filled with aer. In the ordinary parlance aer belonged to the region of corruption, decay, and mortality. Aer was the sublunary atmosphere, and in the upper part of aer the daimons dwelt. The air that we breathe, fog, mist, cloud, and even darkness, all can be represented by the same word aer. On the other hand, the root meaning of aither is "blazing," and aither etymologically suggests "fine." The Olympian Greeks had thought that the top of Mountain Olympus was high enough to reach out from the impure atmosphere (aer) into the divine and immaterial element of aither. In this clear blue sky on the top of Mountain Olympus the gods were said to live.

Now we turn to their cognizance of the identity of the divine being. This had to do with the origins of the Olympian gods. The Olympian gods rose out of an animistic outlook on nature. They are a sort of personification of some of the daimons. A few examples might suffice to illustrate this point. The same Greek word boreas is the

15

name of the north wind and of the legendary
being supposed to govern the north wind. The
god of the sky and weather, Zeus, is declined
in more than one way, and among the resulting
forms are an accusative, Dia, and a by-form
of the nominative, Zen or Zm. These happen
to sound like the Greek words for "through"
(dia) and "live" (zeh) respectively. Hence
it has been often assumed that he was thus
named because he was the power through whom
things happen or which gives life. The god
of the messengers, Hermes, is connected with
herma, which means stone ballast, and implied
"he from the stone-heap." In a country
without roads the cairns served the
landmarks, and in the cairn a daimon was said
to reside. Since the cairn was a landmark,
this daimon became a guide and a protector of
the traveller. Since it also was a
grove-mound, he became the guide of souls,
showing them the way to their destiny.

Thus the simple need helped them see the
things of nature in a more concrete form. It
now is very clear that the deepest needs of
the ancient Greeks created the Olympian gods.
Also, the analogy between the human child
coming from the seed laid in his mother's
womb and the grain germinating from the seed
laid in the ground was presented to their
mind, and took expression of Demeter. De is
a by-form of the word for spelt, the inferior
grain, and meter, "mother." Thus Demeter is
the spelt-mother, or corn-mother, and became
the goddess of agriculture. Her daughter
Kore (Persephone) is the divine equivalent of
the new grain that is stored away.

In the process of personification of the
natural forces and daimons, when high culture
was introduced and man was set above the
animals, anthropomorphism introduced itself.
Anthropomorphism is a manner of visualization
of the gods. The Olympians began to think of
their gods as possessing human shape and a
nature like that of man. This thought seemed

to have emerged out of a common belief that both gods and mankind were fashioned in the same mold from the same primogenitor, and were children of Earth (Gaia). Behind this belief there was a myth of the birth of Zeus and Dionysus Zeagreus.[13]

In the myth of Zeus' birth, Rheu, wife of Kronos, was about to bear another child. Her parents, Ouranos and Gaia sent her to Crete. There she bore Zeus. In the myth of Dionysus Zeagreus, Zeagreus was the son of Zeus and Perspephone. In her jealousy Hera, another wife of Zeus, sent the Titans to destroy Zeagreus. After a struggle, they managed to kill Zeagreus, cut him up, and devoured all but the heart, which was saved by Athena and carried to Zeus. Zeus swallowed it up, and produced thereof another son, Dionysus. Zeus destroyed the Titans by lightening, and from the ashes of the Titans he created man. Man is thus composed of two elements, one bad, the Titanic, and the other good, the Dionysiac. In the manner both gods and mankind traced their origin back to this common source.

By virtue of having the same primogenitor, man resembles gods in his essential being. But the Olympians recognized enormous differences between gods and man. The gods suffered from neither old age nor death. In their undecaying strength and beauty the gods had something denied to men. Between them also lies an immeasurable difference of power in their experience. The distinguishing quality of their gods was perceived in power above everything. They believed that, although men could form something like friendship with gods, it was not a friendship between equals. If men presumed too much on it, they would have to pay the penalty. When a certain Niobe boasted that her children were as beautiful as Leto's, they were destroyed by Apollo and Artemis. When

17

Pentheus, king of Thebes, mocked and imprisoned Dionysus, he was torn to pieces by the
Bacchants who worshiped Dionysus.[14]

Their gods were moved by consideration of
personal honor, and anything which might be
construed as an affront to it, excited their
anger and called for violent vengeance.
Forgiveness was not in their nature, and once
a man had offended them, he had no excuse and
could expect no mercy. In their jealousy of
their own honor, the gods also might humble
men who were too prosperous and enjoyed more
happiness than is fit for mortals. Too much
success and prosperity were insecure because
their gods disliked them. This had
strengthened the doctrine of mean.

Nonetheless, the average Greeks had taken
a very optimistic attitude toward their gods.
One of the commenest epithets that the gods
had received from them was "giver of good."
"Good" was what was expected of them. The
Olympians normally trusted in the general
justice and kindness of their gods. They
called their gods savior. The salvation the
Greeks looked for, however, was of a purely
material kind, the protection of community
and, to somewhat lesser degree, of individuals from the physical dangers of political
and individual life. The ordinary Olympians
had addressed themselves to the gods only in
their present needs. This is demonstrated in
the characterization of their gods'
function.[15]

Zeus was characterized as the cloud-
gatherer who sent the rain, the lightening,
and the thunder. Poseidon was the god of
water in general, of rivers and springs. As
the water-god he concerned with the earth,
which cannot be fruitful if it is dry.
Apollo was the god of law and order, and of
interpretation. Everything that connects
with law and interpretation was his concern.

18

In order to learn the will of the gods, the Olympians consulted the oracles of Apollo at Delphi. Apollo also had exegetai, "interpreters," through whom he gave advice both to the city-states and to private citizens. Ares, a warrior god, loved the fighting for the sake of fighting. Hephaistos, the god of fire, was the patron of craftsman, especially of smith, armours, and cunning workers in gold and silver. Hermes, "he of the stonepile," was the patron of heralds and sent messages on public business from one community to another. His messages were regarded as inviolable, even in time of war. The rest of the Olympian deities, the six goddesses, were also assigned to the appropriate spheres of function and duty: Hera, the goddess of marriage; Athena, of wisdom and civilization; Artemis, a mother-goddess; Aphrodite, of love, beauty and of fertility; Demeter, of Agriculture; and Hestia, of family life.

On the other hand, the Olympian Greeks quite frequently had to face a tension between their trust in general justice and kindness of the gods, and the calamities and many adversities in their public and private lives. When anything unexpected happened, they were liable either to feel wants, or to confront the problem of why the good who presumably are well-pleasing to the gods do not always prosper. But they seemed to have positively worked out the tension, especially from a common belief in fate.

Many unexpected things, over which an ordinary person had neither understanding nor control, were likely to take place in communal and private lives. Under the circumstance, many resorted to a belief in a blind and capricious power, and had a vague hope that they might be able to induce that power to their favor.

Two things might have promoted the belief in fate. One was concerned with a general mentality. Everywhere man had always believed in luck or chance (tyche), good or bad. By "chance" we mean something of which causes we can neither control, predict, nor understand. The other was the certain "lot" (moira) of every man, that is, death. Death had been regarded as man's regular portion in life above all else. Every man expects the coming of his death, and this expectation exerted so powerful an influence that it was said that not even the gods can avert it. Under this influence, individual death had been regarded as predetermined and was assigned simultaneously with his birth. From this thought eventually arose fatalism. Its root was the inevitability of death. Just as death is man's lot, and is assigned upon the day of birth, so the idea arose that the whole course of life had been predetermined at birth. Finally a general conviction emerged that everything does not always go as one would wish, as it was already predetermined, and that everything should work for him in accordance with his "portion" or "lot."

Still, the individual Greek had been generally, in some small measure at least, the arbiter of his own destiny. He could approach his gods for their help and informaton on anything concerned with his daily life. He believed that any god might send a warning sign or signs. The gods were said to inform mankind through various omens, especially the cries and flights of the birds of prey, of coming events. Hence the name for this kind of bird, ornis, came to mean "omen."[16]

A traditional science of augury was as old as Homer's day. The people had tried to discover what was to happen, and especially whether any enterprises were likely to succeed or fail. Also the consultants went to a god's statue in the temple in the evening, filled and lit the lamps which stood before the statue, burned incence in the hearth, laid a bronze piece of the local coinage on the altar, and whispered his question into the ear of the image. Then stopping his own ears with his fingers, he left the temple, and as soon as he had gotten outside the market place where the shrine stood, he unstopped his ears and listened to the talk of any chance passer-by. The words he overheard were his answer. It had been a general belief that on occasion ordinary people were permitted to use words which meant more than they knew, and that it was Hermes who put the words into the minds of those about the temple to mention. This sort of divination was called the kledon, "fortune telling."

When he had an urgent need, he could make special entreaty to his gods. This entreaty usually was not accompanied by confession of shortcomings, promise of amendment or repentance, but it was simply a special appeal for help. In order to increase the divine power (mana), he usually offered sacrifice to his gods, and his sacrifices were meant to be the offering of the life of the victim to increase the divine power and to enable his gods to answer the entreaty and prayers. In the past, however, sacrifices had been made to placate anger and inscrutable gods. But in time sacrifices had become a feast, at which both the gods and the votaries shared the same pleasure. On the one hand, the sacrifices had served the pur- pose of increasing divine power, and on the other hand, they promoted the act of hop- sitality among the votaries.

21

The Shintoists

An ordinary Shintoist, like the ancient Babylonians and the Olympian Greeks, takes a neutral attitude toward life hereafter. His main concern and interest are with the present earthly life, which is said under the influence of kami, a "spirit." Kami,[17] theoretically speaking, is anything that possesses an unusual quality or potency and is capable of conveying the sacredness. It may refer to the quality itself in an object, and it is definitely associated with animism. Anything can be regarded as a kami; spirits of ancestors, heroes of the past, and emperors are believed to be the special kamis. The kamis are supposed to work their power through ramat, which is something analogous to mana. Some of the kamis are good, and some are evil, and some are remote, distant, and inaccessible. But many of kamis are familiar and accessible, with whom the Japanese think they can have a communion.

The idea of kami has been long a part of the traditional Japanese culture ever since pre-historic times, going back to the era before Japan had established a contact with China. At that time the way of life on earth was thought to be the way of kami. This is clearly expressed in the old Japanese word for government, matsuri-goto. Matsuri is a shrine observance or celebration, and goto means "thing." Government, that is, matsuri-goto, means "shrine observance thing" or "attending to kami affairs." The implication here is not that heaven directs earthly affairs but that man is heavenly spirit on earth, and that all life and the entire universe are spirit-kami. The idea of kami was also noticed in another old Japanese word, kami-no-michi. The syllable mi is a sacred title "august" or divine, and chi is a very old Japanese word for "way." Michi thus implies "divine way" and kami-no-michi is understood as "the kami divine way" or "kami-ism."

When Japan adopted Chinese culture and language, the Chinese word shinto[18] replaced kami no michi and has become the general term for it. The syllable "to" in shinto is derived from tao. The ancient Chinese ideograph for tao was a crossroad with hairs in the center representing the severed head of a criminal. This ideograph expresses the idea that a man at the crossroad must choose his own way. To the syllable "to" the Chinese character shin, meaning kami, was prefixed to create the word shinto, "the way of kami." In result, shinto means kami-man at the crossroad choosing his own way.

Although we can trace the beginning of Shintoism or kami-no-michi to the era of the Jomon-Ainu pre-historic culture, the essence of Shintoism can be grasped from two Japanese classics, Kojiki and Nihongi,[19] which were compiled in the early eighth century A.D. In these classics, when goddess Isanami died she went down to the land of darkness, called yomi, and her male consort Isanagi followed her. But it was too late, because she had already begun to decay, so that Isanagi was overcome with horror and fled from the sight of death and corruption. Escaping from the land of darkness, his first care was to purify himself by bathing in the sea. From this mythical purification a central theme of Shintoism had been evolved: pollution and purification.

The things that cause pollution and are offensive before kami are called tsumi, "guilt" or "sin," and avoidance of these things are called imi, "taboo." There also emerged a class of professional "abstainers," imibe, whose duty was to keep free from pollution, so that they might be in a state of purity to approach kami without offence.

Tsumi in general are in two categories, the heavenly offences and the earthly offences. The former were those offences committed by one of the kamis, Susa-no-wo in heaven against Amaterasu-o-mikami. The latter are killing, desecration of the corpses, leprosy, incest, and so on.

Shintoism, from the beginning, stresses the state of purity.[20] One must be in a state of purity before he could approach to kami for a certain purpose. The water cleansing for ritual purity was introduced, and it is called harai. Harai was to remove the pollution caused by any tsumi, and con-sists of offerings. Another cleansing rite, called misogi, was to remove accidental defilment occuring by contact with unclean things (e.g. the corpse). It is done by absolution or a mere sprinkling of water or salt. Occasionally O harai, "great purification," was performed on behalf of the entire community and nation. The imi, "abstention," is a method of acquiring purity by avoidance of the sources of pollution.

In practical terms, Shintoism, "the way of kami," is preparation for the earthly life and mundane affairs. In it there is no idea of retribution beyond the present earthly life. The Shintoists do not speculate and have concern with life hereafter. They regard life as a realm in which both kami and man seek to purify themselves by means of self-cleansing. They never offer prayers, because prayers are petitions from humanity to a deity. The Shinto priests recite norito, but norito are forms of paying respect and expressing gratitude to kami for their help. Like the ancient Babylonians and Greeks, they believe in a continual existence in an abode of the dead, in the depth of the earth. But their main concern is how to maintain peace and good will with kami for the prosperity and the welfare of the

community. This can be achieved only when
purity is maintained through ritual cleansing
and purification. They have no reason to
fear and be concerned about their future,
because they believe that their future is
already secured in the gloomy place in the
depth of the earth.

NOTES

Chapter 1

1. W.W.F. Saggs, The Greatness that was Babylon (New York: Hawthorn Books, 1963), p. 302.

2. Henri Frankfort, et al, Before Philosophy (Baltimore: Penguin books, 1964), pp. 13-14, 142.

3. Saggs, op. cit., pp. 305-306.

4. Ibid., pp. 328 ff.; Samuel Noah Kramer, Mythologies of the Ancient World (Garden City: Anchor Books, 1961), pp. 96 ff.; Frankfort, et al, op. cit., pp. 148 ff.

5. Ibid., pp. 11 ff.; James B. Pritchard (Ed.), Ancient Near Eastern Texts (Princeton: Princeton University Press, 1955), pp. 52-57; 106-110.

6. Georges Contenau, Everyday Life in Babylon and Assyria (London: Edward Arnold, 1959), p. 199.

7. Pritchard, op. cit., pp. 60-72; Alexandria Heidel, The Babylonian Genesis (Chicago: The University of Chicago Press, 1950), pp. 3 ff.

8. Pritchard, op. cit., pp. 72 ff.; N.K. Sanders, The Epic of Gilgamesh (Baltimore: Penguin books, 1964) pp. 59 ff.

9. Pritchard, op. cit. pp. 101-103.

10. Charles Seltman, The Twelve Olympians (New York: Thomas Y. Crowell Company, 1962), pp. 31 ff.

11. Jane Harrison, Themis (London: Merlin Press, 1977) pp. 260 ff.; Kramer, op. cit., pp. 228 ff.

12. Martin Persson Nilsson, A History of Greek Religion (Oxford: The Clarendon Press, 1963), pp. 134 ff.

13. Harrson, op. cit., pp. 13 ff.

14. H.J. Rose, Religion in Greece and Rome (New York: Harper and Brothers, 1959), pp. 60-62; Nilsson, op. cit., pp. 205-210; 293-294.

15. W.K.C. Guthrie, The Greeks and their Gods (Boston: Beacon Press, 1956), pp. 35 ff.

16. Harrison, op. cit., pp. 98-99; 415 ff.

17. Sokgo Ono, Shinto the Kami Way (Bridgeway Press, 1962), pp. 6-7; J.W.T. Mason, the Meaning of Shinto (Port Washington: Kennikat Press), pp. 49ff; Jean Herbert, Shinto (New York: Stein and Day, 1967), pp. 23-24.

18. Ono, op. cit., pp. 2-4; Mason, op. cit., pp. 56ff.

19. Nihongi, trans. W.G. Aston (London: George Allen and Unwin LTD, 1956).

20. Mason, op. cit., pp. 86ff; Ono, op. cit., pp. 102ff; Herbert, op. cit., pp. 79-82; 84ff.

Chapter II

The Circular Eschatology

In view of the historic-terminal eschatology, the present world serves as the end in itself and is always becoming the state of consummation to every individual, beyond which there is nothing to look for. On the other hand, the circular eschatology sees the present world as merely a prelude to the state of consummation and the means to the end. In the religious dimension, the cause-effect relationship comes in, and the present moment of life becomes the antecedent and the causal determinative of another in a series of lives. One life in this series of incarnations is usually commensurate with hope in ascending degree for the achievement of the end toward which one given life might move one step further.

The series of lives, "reincarnations" or "rebirths," with the self realization, has become the fundamental tenet of the circular eschatology. The self-realization had been variously named: nirvana, moksha, or the integration of atman, for example. Both the self-realization and reincarnation are the processes which had to take place in life on earth. At the moment of the achievement of the self-realization, the series of reincarnations should come to an end. This thought has been expressed with different degrees of articulation and in different forms by the Orphic Greeks, the Hindus, and Buddhists.

The Orphics

We include among the Orphics the ancient Greeks who practiced Orphism and also who had developed the philosophic-religious ideas in

29

the Orphic line. Orpheus[1] was regarded
by the ancient Greeks as the founder of a
certain kind of religion, which among modern
scholars called Orphism, after his name.
According to Conon and Strabo's witnesses,
Orpheus was the son of a muse, Kalliope being
most often mentioned as his mother. His
father is sometimes said to be Apollo, though
more often Oiagros, a Thracian river-god.
Leaving some doubt as to whether he was
Thracian or Macedonian in origin, he was at
one point in his career a Thracian and a
magical musician. Modern scholarship still
leaves his origin unsettled. Nor has a definite position on his death been settled.
Some in the classical writings said he was
slain by Zeus because he, like Prometheus,
revealed mysteries to man. According to
Plato, he was bound up with his descent to
the underworld after his wife, Eurydice,[2]
who was killed by a bite of a snake.
Orpheus, after wandering in disconsolation,
turned vainly to his lyre for solace, and
descended at last through the gate of
Tainaron to the realm of the dead to bring
Eurydice back to the upper realm. But the
gods of the underworld sent him back empty
handed, because he was only a poor-spirited
musician who tried to get down to Hades alive
instead of dying for the love of Eurydice.
He was said to have resumed his wandering
disconsolatly and playing his lyre for
solace. He eventually attracted many
men, and their women murdered him being
moved by jealousy because he excluded them
from his rite and enticed their husbands away
from them.

Orpheus appeared, whatever his origin
might have been, in history as a human
prophet and teacher, whose teaching was
embodied in a collection of writings, the
"Rhapsodic Theogony."[3] This collection is a
poem in twenty-four cantos, the substance of
which was drawn from earlier writings current

in various communities. These writings had
shown that he did not have a new and entirely
distinct species of religion to offer, but a
modification of religion. His teaching was
mainly concerned with immortality, posthumous
rewards and punishment, reincarnation, and
ritual purification. The basic foundation of
his teaching of these issues, however, is the
doctrine of the nature of man. In his
teachings of the nature of man we notice he
was influenced by the common myth of Zagreus.

The myth of Zagreus[4], which had also
received the name "Orphic mystery," deals
with good and evil. According to this myth,
in the series of divine generation the age of
Zeus arrives. Among the children of Zeus the
greatest is Orphic Dionysos, also known as
Zagreus, whom Zeus had designated to succeed
himself in the rule of the world. The
Titans, who had strived to recover the dominion for themselves, lured Zagreus into their
power, killed and devoured him. Only his
heart, saved by Athena, lived again in the
third Dionysos, the son of Zeus and Semele.
Zeus consumed the Titans with fire from
heaven and scattered their ashes to the
winds. But through the cannibal beast, the
essence of Dionysos (Zagreus) had entered
into the Titans themselves, and the wind-
borne ashes convey the germ of the divine
life into all animate things. At last man
was created out of the ashes of the Titans,
and in this manner man received a dual
nature, Dionysos-Zagreus and Titanic, the
divine and demonic natures.

Accordingly, the chief end of man for the
Orphics was to rid himself of the Titanic
element and preserve the Dionysiac, divine,
element in his complex being. Before him in
this world lies a long series of lives, and
during each of them he may be rewarded or
punished for good or evil deeds wrought in
his previous life. In the end he may attain

31

to something like the divine and eternal. In order to attain the ultimate end, the Orphics must follow through the "Orphic life" which is a mixture of ceremonies and abstinences.

Orphism laid its stress upon ritual purity[5], if the immortality and the divinity of human soul were not to be forfeited. This ritual purity also was necessary not only on certain occasions, but also throughout life for the elimination of the Titanic element in human nature and for the achievement of the ultimate end.

Before one could reach the ultimate end, he had to complete at least ten times the series of reincarnations.[6] A soul dies, is judged and assigned to a place of punishment or happiness. Whatever it is, the sojourn is temporary, and he completed 1,000 years and then reincarnates for another life on earth. All souls destined for reincarnation were made to drink a certain amount of the water of Lethe to make them forget their experiences in the other world. After drinking the water of Lethe, they were to be born to the body either human or animal. They were to complete ten times this "weary circle" before salvation could be hoped for.

At the first reincarnation, it was the law that a soul entered the body of man and not a beast. But he became a different type of man, lower or higher. The souls, after the first life, were judged, and some went to the underworld, while others went to heaven. When the millennium was about to be over, they had to choose a second life. At this point it was possible for the soul of a man to become that of a beast and the soul of a beast to become that of a man. There was, however, some exception to this law. He who was being justified by carrying out the "Orphic life" went through the "weary circle" only three times and escaped without further trial. On the last reincarnation, souls were to be born into the highest type of man, and after the last reincarnation they at last sprang forth as divine.

Plato had a great interest in the Orphic idea of reincarnation and philosophized it to set forth the doctrine of metempsychosis or transmigration of soul.[7] When Plato set forth his doctrine of transmigration in the Orphic reasoning, first he attempted to prove, on the grounds of epistemological and metaphysical (Phaedeo) and valuational-moral (Republic) arguments, the immortality of the human soul. He epistemologically argued that a soul, that has contemplated the pure and eternal ideas, must, at least in part, be like those ideas, pure and eternal, because only like can know like. His metaphysical argument in essence comprised two sets of arguments, the argument from the unity and simplicity of the soul, and the argument from the vitality of the soul. Plato regarded the soul as simple and indivisible by nature. It can, therefore, neither be produced by composition nor be destroyed by disintegration. Since the soul is a principle of life, it would be, Plato further argued, a contradiction to suppose that the principle of life should die. He inferred from this step that life can't become death, and so the soul should be immortal.

Plato's valuational-moral argument implies that the world, being conceived as a moral, rational, and just order, demands a future life of reward and punishment for the rectification of imperfection of this life.

After having argued for the immortality of the human soul, Plato had recourse to a mythical explanation for the union between soul and body.[8] According to him, the soul is a purely spiritual being, uncreated

33

(Phaedeo) and eternal (Republic). The soul
in its pre-existence was the entity of a
trichotomy of reason, courage, and desire.
He explained its fall by the presence of the
latter two. However, we observe that he
modified it later by saying that it was not
until a soul was enclosed in the body that
courage and desire were associated with it,
these being proper to the body only. Having
been impregnated with a desire for the world
of sense, the soul was imprisoned in a
material body as in a prison. Had the soul
resisted desire in its celestial life, the
soul would have continued to enjoy a
transcendent existence. Since it has failed
in this, it was condemned to pass through a
stage of transmigration for purification.

The transmigration of the soul is of
necessity the factor in view of the Orphics
and platonists. It had become discipline of
the soul, and in this phase Hades becomes an
intermediate abode where the soul meets with
retributive judgment. There the initiated
and purified live in communion with the gods
of the lower world till the time for return
to the upper life has come. At last the soul
has been translated into a pure intelligence
or idea.

The pure intelligence or idea comprehends
or holds together the essential qualities
common to many particulars. It is not mere
thought in the mind of a man, but is said to
be substance, real, and original, and the
eternal transcendent archetype of things
existing prior to things and apart from them.
The particulars may come and go, but the
ideas go on forever. For instance, men may
come and go, but the man-type is eternal.
Ideas subsume under the highest idea, the idea
of the good which is the source of all the
rest. The Platonic ideas thus are non-mental
and non-temporal, as well as non-spatial. They
are of necessity eternal and immutable. But

Plato asserted that the pure intelligence or idea had become contaminated with earthly and corporeal "matter," and that the dualism of soul and body in human being resulted. The soul can't immediately shake off the "matter" element at death to ascend to the upper realm, but engages the series of transmigrations.

Plato had worked his idea of the redemption of the human soul on the ground of the "form-matter" paradoxy, transcendentalism between form and matter.[9] Aristotle, however, had brought the Platonic idea down to earth; form and matter are no longer at the poles of the universe apart, but are united in individual objects. According to Aristotle, above the universe there is pure form (idea), pure actuality, pure thought, the unmoved prime mover, the final cause of all becoming, that is, a god. The Stoics made a further step to arrive at monism, and brought the unmoved prime mover or a god back from his banishment, and they made him a immanent being in every part of the universe. On the ground of this monism the Stoics expounded the same issue of the union of body and soul and the redemption of the soul.

The Stoics comprehended the universe as a living, intelligent being, by virtue of the fact that the final cause of all becoming, that is, a god pervades it to the smallest particle, like the human soul in the body.[10] The final cause is a spiritual being, consisting of two finer elements of fire and vapour. This spirit presents itself everywhere, but in different degrees of purity and fineness, imparts to all things their distinctive qualities, holds them together, and sets them in motion. As there is one force, so there is one universal causal nexus, the universal soul or logos, running through the entire universe. Thus Stoics had seen that the cosmic process

35

including the union of body and soul was the evolution of the one primeval substance, which is a purposeful intelligence, the universal logos.[11]

This universal soul (logos) is something what the Hindus call atman. The individual soul is a part of the evolved cosmos and capable of living in harmony with the universal soul; it is a part of the universal soul, permeated in our body. Thus, in the view of the Stoics, the union of the body and soul is a cosmic union, not a sort of imprisonment of the soul in the human body as the Platonists understood it. Having a similar presupposition on this issue, the Stoics had reached the Hindic conclusion on the matter of the ultimate end of life. What is the Stoics ultimate end of life? The answer to this question is given in our next discussion on the Hindu-Buddhists' circular eschatology.

The Hindu-Buddhists

As we traverse eastward from ancient Greece through the Mesopotamian Valley to India and the Far East, we find the typical circular eschatology among the Hindus and the Buddhists. Bharat is the ancient name of India, which is derived from the legendary king Bharat. Bharat established the first dynasty to rule over the then-known area of India, namely, the Indus Valley. The names Indian and Hindu, however, are derived from the Sanskrit name for the great river Sindhu, which flows through western India, now a part of Pakistan. The Greeks called the river Indus and the country around it India. The Persians called the region Hindustan and the people dwelling there Hindus. The Hindus are a mixed race of the Indo-Aryans and the Dravidians, who were the most numerous indegenous group at the time when the Indo-Aryans pressed down into the northern plains of India during the years of 2000-1000 B.C.

36

The most important source of our
knowledge about the Indo-Aryan and Dravidian
racial fusion is the sacred wisdom
literature, Veda.[12] The word Veda derives
from vid, "to know," and means knowledge par
excellence. The Veda is not a single
literary work, or a collection of a number of
books, but a whole literature which arose
over the centuries and was handed down from
generation to generation by word of mouth.
It was declared to be the sacred knowledge
and divine revelation. As a result, it has
become the standard of thought and feeling
for the Indians. The common usage is to
classify this ancient literature into four
Vedas: Rig, Yaju, Sama, and Atharva. The
oldest and the most important of these is the
Rigveda, of which only one recension came
down to us, consisting of 1,028 hymns. The
next important Veda is the Atharva; the
Atharva contains a large number of magical
formulae. The Sama consists of a large
number of Rik mantras and is in general use
for singing. The Yajurveda deals with the
works of sacrifice.

Along with these Vedas, the Hindus
possess a number of sacred scriptures
including the Itiharas and the Puranas.[13]
The word Itiharas means "epics," and it is
made up of two works, called the Mahabharata
and the Ramayana. The Mahabharata, which is
the longest poem in the world, contains
100,000 couplets. The most famous part of
this epic is the Bhagavad-Gita, "the Lord's
Song," of some 700 verses.[14] This is the
most beloved Hindu literature and is a piece
of profound philosophy in poetic form. The
poem is in the form of a reported conver-
sation between Arjuna, the great warrior, and
his charioteer, Krishna, who is the incarnation of the Supreme. The warrior's
conscience revolts at the thought of war and
the large scale murder it involves. He conveys his distress to Krishna. Krishna

replies that as a warrior he must do his
duty; then he moves on to a discussion of the
problem of individual duty and of social
behavior.

The Ramayana is based on the life of
Rama, who also was the prophet and the incarnation of the Supreme. This poem deals
mainly with domestic development, with the
wandering of the hero and the dutiful stead-
fastness of his wife, Sita. Sita had given
up a comfortable home life and followed her
husband, Rama, into a jungle exile. She was
then kidnapped by the demon-king of Ceylon.
After being rescued, to prove her innocence,
she threw herself into a great fire, but the
fire rejected her. Thus she was proven
innocent. Still she suffered banishment and
social ostracism. In spite of this unjust
treatment, Sita remained thoroughly a sub-
missive and obedient wife to Rama.

The Puranas are the heroic stories of
kings and common people, prophets, and
saints. Another important sacred writing is
the Upanishads. The word "upanisad" is
derived from upa, "near," ni, "down," and
sad "to sit," and thus it means sitting down
near. Groups of pupils sit near the teacher
to learn from him the secret knowledge. The
Upanishads contain accounts of the mystic
significance of the syllable Aum, which is
intelligible only to the initiated, and
secret esoteric doctrine, and discussion of
the ultimate reality, called Brahman.

Brahman[15] is something like a pure
intelligence or idea in the platonists'
terminology, or the Stoics' universal soul
(logos). As early as the Vedic period
(2000-1000 B.C.), the Hindu thinkers had spoken of the absolute, acosmic or transcendental and unconditioned Brahman, and the
relative, cosmic or phenomenal and conditioned Brahman. They had begun to articu-

38

late their experience with the ultimate reality from two different dimensions of cognition, that is, monistic and one unitary, and pluralistic perceptions. In the Vedas, Brahman is described as the first principle. From it all things are derived, and in this sense it is a creator Brahma; by it all are supported, and in this sense it is a protector Vishnu; and into it finally all are absorbed, and in this sense it is a destroyer or preserver Siva. Here they had addressed themselves from the pluralistic perception to the phenomenal and conditioned Brahman. Along with the conditioned Brahman in the Vedas, we are aware of the transcendental and unconditioned Brahman; in it alone the apparent differences of the phenomenal world are unified.

The Upanishads also speak of the transcendental Brahman as devoid of qualifying attributes and indicative marks, and of the phenomenal Brahman as endowed with the qualifying attributes. The traitless Brahman is called the Supreme or unconditioned Brahman, and the other inferior or conditioned Brahman. The former is further described as the one divine Being "hidden in all beings, all pervading, the self (atman) within all beings." The Hindu philosphers often expound the identity of the unconditioned Brahman in terms of Satchidananda, "pure existence-knowledge-bliss."

Here the word "existence" indicates that Brahman is not non-existence. But Brahman does not exist as an empirical object, but rather as absolute existence. No object, illusory or otherwise, could exist without the foundation of an immutable existence, and that existence is said to be Brahman. The substratum of the universe is said to be Brahman. The word "existence," therefore, as applied to Brahman, suggests the negation of both empirical reality and its correlative, unreality.

In the Upanishads Brahman and Atman
("self") are the same. In the Vedas the
identification of the two is expressed in the
formula of "that thou art." Thus
Brahman is the knowing subject within man.
It is the inner "knowledge" and consciousness
and the real agent of perception. Because
Brahman is, in reality, Atman, it is
consciousness, knowledge or intelligence in
the Platonic sense. It is regarded as self-
luminous and needs no other light to illumine
itself.

The third aspect of Satchidananda is
"bliss." Brahman is bliss because it is
knoweldge or intelligence, so the Hindus
reasoned. They reasoned that no real bliss
is possible without knowledge, and that
Brahman is bliss because of the absence of
duality in it. They saw every evil as being
caused by the consciousness of duality.
Futhermore, they reasoned that Brahman is
bliss because it is infinite and that there
is no real and enduring joy in the finite.

By means of its own inscrutable power,
called maya,[16] the unconditioned Brahman
becomes the conditioned Brahman who is now
endowed with the attributes of a personal
god, and manifests itself in multiple forms,
including Brahma, Vishnu, and Siva.

Maya is a sort of magical power, by means
of which Brahman projects the universe, like
a magician producing two or more coins from
one. In modern time Ramakriskna worhsipped
maya as the divine mother, who holds in her
womb all living beings, and who, like a
mother, supports them after creating them,
and, at the end of the cycle, withdraws them
into herself. In general, maya is viewed as
a supreme power compounded of three gunas,
which are its stuff and are the three strands
that constitute the substance of maya. These

gunas are called rajas, tamas, and suttva.
Rajas and tamas are in opposition, while
suttva strikes a balance between the two.
The main trait of rajas is energy, and its
visible effect is seen in ceaseless activity.
Tamas manifests itself as inactivity, while
Suttva reveals itself with spiritual qualities and is characterized by balance. When
the equilibrium is disturbed, on account of
one guna preponderance, there takes place the
creation of the material universe. Maya is
thus a sort of the Aristotelian material
cause, and Brahman, as pure intelligence, is
the efficient cause.

After having projected all material
forms, including our mind, Brahman enters
them as life and consciousness, and animates
them. In this manner the transcendental and
unconditioned Brahman becomes immanent in the
universe, and is subject to man's perception
and is conceived as the conditioned Brahman
and a personal god.

The unique manifestation of the unconditioned Brahman is the avatara, incarnation
of god. To the Christians, the incarnation
is limited to one historical personage, Jesus
Christ. But, on the conrary, the Hindus do
not impose any limitation or time or place.
The word avatara means "the descent of the
lord into the world of man and animals," and
it occurs to fulfill a cosmic need whenever
such a need arises.

The Vedas also discussed the nature of
Atman, "self," from the absolute or
transcendental, and the relative or phenomenal points of view. From the absolute-
transcendental point of view, atman is
non-real, immortal, ever pure, ever free, and
one with Brahman. Atman in this point of
view is "supreme soul" (paramatma). From the
relative phenomenal point of view, atman is

individual soul (jivatmas) that is entangled and attached to the body.

The union of body and soul thus was regarded as being effected in the same way as the unconditioned Brahman is becoming the conditioned Braham. In association with the same maya the absolute-transcendental atman is becoming the individual soul or jiva. The conditioned Brahman and the individual soul or jiva are the manifestation of the absolute Brahman on the relative plane. There is, however, some distinction between the two. The differences are the result of the fact that the conditioned Brahman keeps maya under its control, whereas the jiva is under maya's control. The jiva is the worshiper, whereas the conditioned Brahman is the object of worship, a personal god.

The Upanishads distinguished between a real self, Isvara-atman, and an apparent self, jiva. The apparent self experiences pain and pleasure as the result of its own acts, good or bad. But the real self is serene and undisturbed, because it is not attached to the world. When the apparent self realizes its oneness with the real self, its grief passes away. Vedic statement, "that thou art," expresses this oneness.

So far what we have said about Brahman and Atman on the two different dimensions, transcendental and phenomenal, could be well illustrated in the following simple diagram:

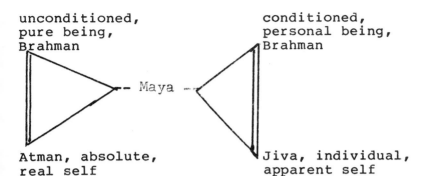

acosmic, transcendental, numenal

cosmic, immanent, phenomenal

unconditioned, pure being, Brahman

conditioned, personal being, Brahman

Maya

Atman, absolute, real self

Jiva, individual, apparent self

It is quite interesting to observe the way that the Vedic philosophers analyzed the realtionship between the real and the apparent selves in our body. They have used five sheaths: the gross physical sheath, the sheath of vital breath (prama), the sheath of the mind, the sheath of the intellect, and the sheath of bliss. Like a sheath concealing an object, these five sheaths conceal the real soul, as being one inside another, the physical sheath being the outermost and the sheath of bliss the innermost. The real self, atman, is inside all the sheaths and permeates them all.

The gross physical sheath is our physical body. Our physical body is changeable by nature, its existence is transitory, and its virtues are ephemeral. Therefore the Hindu thinkers conclude that the body cannot be the real self. However, they place a high value on our physical body. Our body could become an instrument and a help to the real self, just as a house is helpful to one who dwells in it. The sheath of the vital breath enters the body at the time of conception, leaves it at the moment of death, and produces the feeling of hunger and thirst. The sheath of mind creates the notion of diversity of ego, and perceives the phenomenal world to exist as real. The sheath of intellect is "I-consciousness." The final sheath of bliss is deeply absorbed feeling in music or art. Because the real self, atman, is their substratum, these sheaths appear to be real. Through the lack of proper knowledge we are said to identify atman, the real self, with one or more of these sheaths. In this identification the real self is imprisoned in our body.

The Hindus and Buddhists alike have to face, with utmost earnest, the basic eschatological question of how to free the self from the body prison. The question of the freedom of the real self atman is at stake, and is the central issue of the Hindu-Buddhist circular eschatology.

In search for the means of freedom of atman from the body, they came to formulate the doctrine of karma,[17] the law of cause and effect and the transmigration. The doctrine of karma implies that man's present disposition of the real self imprisoned in the body is the result of his past, and that the present action creates his future. Thus a man is the architect of his own destiny and the builder of his own fate. All things are seen in a state of constant flux, and each act leaves its trace on the five constituents which make up a phenomenal individual. The five components of our being are form and matter (rupa), sensation (vedana), perception (shmijna), psychic disposition (samskara), and consciousness (vijnana). When the material and immaterial parts of being are separated in death, the immaterial carries over the consequential effects of the deeds of the past life, and obtains another body accordingly.

The human body has desire of many kinds,
and the embodied real self is bound by
desires. Freedom of the real self from the
body only comes from the absence of desire,
which, according to the Buddhists' term, is
nirvana. The word nirvana means "blowing
out," thus it is "nothingness." In the state
of nirvana all the idea of an individual personality ceases to exist, and there is nothing
to be "nothingness" reborn. According to
Hindu teaching, this can't be attained
without experiencing the futility of all
worldly desires. In the Phenomenal world,
everything is transient and transitory, and
there is nothing real. The human body is the
instrument through which desires are
fulfilled. When it has fulfilled every
desire through the process of rebirth and
repeated lives, without deriving any abiding
satisfaction and finds the relative world to
be transitory and bound by the law of karma,
it at last longs for communion with Brahman,
which is alone untouched by the law of
causation. The nature of our present life
and its duration are said to be determined by
the action and the unfulfilled desires of the
previous life. Freedom of the real self from
the body thus meant salvation, and this
liberation, known as moksha,[18] implies
"emptiness" and "nothingness" in union with
the ultimate reality, that is, the unconditioned Brahman. In other words, moksha is
the realization of atman being liberated from
its attachment to the corporeal entity of the
human body. For the attainment of moksha a
number of means have been worked out.

One of the means of liberation is called
"the path of a progress" or "the progress of
an individual."[19] Our life was conceived as
a journey to the ultimate truth of liberation,
and the life journey is divided into four
successive or progressive stages, called
asramas: the stage of discipline and educa-
tion (brahmacarya), the life of the house

45

holder (garhasthya), the stage of the recluse (vanaprasthya), and the life of a hermit (sannyasa). Each stage has its own responsibility and obligation, and one must be faithful in performance. The first stage covers the period of study, and one devotes himself to study and discipline, and cultivates his mind and prepares himself for service to society. The second stage of the householder begins with marriage. A normal person requires a mate, and his biological and emotional urges in this respect are legitimate. The Hindus regard marriage as a sacred duty and discipline. Husband and wife are co-partners in their spiritual growth. The family is believed to provide a training ground for the practice of unselfishness. Therefore the Hindu now should marry and settle down as a householder and faithfully discharge his duties to his community and his country. Five great duties are prescribed to the householders: the study and teaching of the Vedas, daily worship through the appropriate rituals, gratification of the departed ancestors by offering to their spirits food and drink, kindness toward domestic animals, and hospitality to guests, the homeless, and the destitute.

The third stage of the recluse begins with old age, and now he withdraws from the world to devote himself to study and meditation on a god. After this period he moves on to the last stage of religious mendicant who renounces the world, all earthly possessions and ties. During this final stage the disciplined life attains its full blossoming.

The path of progress as a discipline is based on the cosmic progress. The Hindu philosophers had seen the universe going through successive stages, beginning with matter and passing through life, consciousness, and intelligence, to spiritual bliss or perfection. Thus their universe is a living organ. At one end of the cosmic scale there is pure matter in which spirit lies dormant, and at the other end is pure spirit in which matter lies dormant. This is very much like the Platonic form and matter scheme of the cosmos, and it is also similar to the Chinese Yin and yang cosmic principles.[20] Between the two extremes there are various orders of dual beings composed partly of matter and partly of spirit. Spirit becomes richer as it ascends the scale, and matter becomes poorer. The spirit appears as life in vegetables, as consciousness in animals, as intelligence in man, and as bliss or perfection in the Supreme Spirit--Brahman--Atman.

Thus between the two extremes of the cosmic scale there is a process of spiritual progress and ascent from matter to life, from life to consciousness, to intelligence, and to bliss. The most important part of the progress is the path of progress in human life which through the four stages of life transfers man to the ultimate reality, liberation (moksha).

Along with this cosmic progress the so-called "four legitimate desires" -- dharma, artha, kama, and moksha -- had become the religious and ethical basis of the path of progress toward liberation, as well as the means of liberation.[21] The fourth desire, moksha, is regarded as the supreme value, and the fulfillment of the first three paves the way toward moksha, "freedom" or "liberation." The Hindus believe that the suppression of the legitimate desires lead to an unhealthy state of mind, and delays the attainment of liberation.

The first legitimate desire, dharm, which is derived from a root meaning "to support," suggests the law of inner growth, by which a person is supported. A person's dharm should not be imposed by society, but be something

47

with which he is born. Dharma is a sort of code of honor, and determines our proper attitude toward the outside world and governs our mental and physical reponses in a given situation. Hinduism stresses that one must follow his own dharma and should not try to imitate a dharma of another.

The second legitimate desire, artha, "wealth," is regarded as indispensible in the present state of society. The wealth must be, however, earned according to dharma; otherwise it debases a man by making him greedy and cruel. The third legitimate desire, kama, is the enjoyment of sense pleasure. This covers a vast area, from the enjoyment of conjugal love to the appreciation of art, music, or poetry. The Hindus recognize that life becomes drab and grey unless one cultivates aesthetic sensitivity, which the Hindus severely condemned.

The ordinary Hindus hold the view that wealth earned and sense pleasure pursued in accordance with dharma become only the legitimate means to an end. They strongly believe that man is in essence spirit (atman), and can't be permanently satisfied with worldly experience. After fulfilling all his worldly desires in accordance with dharma, he should still want to know the real source of happiness and satisfaction. At last he gives up attachment to the world and seeks freedom from the worldly attachment through the knowledge of the spirit. The genuine desire for freedom from the worldly attachment, thus prompted by the finite view of life, is called moksha, the fourth and the last legitimate desire.

Thus the four legitimate desire imply the principle of the progressive realization of the spirit, atman. At the end of the progression there awaits liberation, moksha. The moksha is clearly conceived as the ulti-

48

mate end of life. Moksha stands for the end of a spiritual progress. But on his way toward this final goal, man has to satisfy the wants of his body and the demands of his society. The wants of his body are what kama expresses and are all the flesh appetites. The demands of his society are what artha conveys. But all these wants and demands have to be met within the limit of the moral law, dharma. How well he pursued dharma in satisfying kama and artha detrmines his destiny in series until he attained moksha. Thus dharma, which usually is translated law, righteousness, duty, or morality, is in essence moksha in the making.

The Hindus also believe that their caste system is originated in conformity with the cosmic law of a spiritual progression, the most spiritual class occupying the top and the least spiritual class the bottom.[22] Accordingly, the caste system had become one of the means of liberation. The Hindu thinkers also acknowledged three fundamental qualities of purity (sattva), energy (rajns), and inertia (tamas), which had determined the four castes. It was supposed that those in whom "purity" predominated formed the Brahmin caste, those in whom "energy" predominated formed the Kshatriya caste, and those in whom inertia predominated in varying degree formed the Vaisaya and Sudra castes. Here we see the law of a progression. Each caste has its own appropriate virtues and obligations. As the Hindus live obediently in accordance with the appropriate virtues, and perform well all the obligations and responsibilities, they can hope for the spiritual progress toward the higher caste, and ultimately for the attainment of moksha.

From what we have observed, it is clear that Hinduism and Buddhism[23] teach that man is the architect of his own destiny. He is the builder of his own future, because his

real self, atman, is divine. Through his
good karma ("action"), the sheaths of his
real self will be eliminated one by one, and
he perceives more and more the divine aspect
of his own self. For its realization, the
Hindus study the scriptures, practice spiritual disciplines, and live joyfully with the
caste system throughout the four stages of
life, and with an earnest effort to satisfy
the legitimate desires within the framework
of dharma.

However, these means just described and
many others do not aim at making a man a perfect human being on earth, but at making him
achieve oneness with the ultimate reality,
the eternal, universal spirit beyond the phenomenal world. With the ultimate
reality,[24] that is, Brahman, there is no
distinction, no cause and effect, no time and
space, no pairs of opposites, and no categories of thought. This ultimate end is said
to be obtained by transforming human
consciousnss into divine consciousness and
not by merely improving human conduct. Since
this transformation is not possible in the
course of a single life, the Hindus and
Buddhists believe in a series of rebirths.

Recognizing the fact that the present
life is only one in the series of rebirths,
and that everyone is in different stages of
the transmigration, the Hindus prescribe a
different discipline which would best suit
one's condition and will enable him to pass
on to the next stage in the progression of
life. Speaking of the spiritual disciplines
categorically, there are three degrees in
descending order of the metaphysical,
religious, and ritual levels. If the
metaphysically oriented discipline is too
advanced and abstract for anyone, the religious discipline is set before him. If he is
not fit for the religious discipline, a
course of ritualitic and moral action is

prescribed for him. At the level of the
religious ideal, the unconditioned Brahman
becomes the conditioned Brahman and a personal god, and the love takes the place of
knowledge. At the ritual ideal, the personal
god is represented by an image, and the rites
and prayers take the place of meditation, and
the religious conduct takes the place of
love.

Let us now turn to another means of
liberation, that is related to the metaphysical ideal, namely, yoga.[25] The word yoga is
cognate with the English word yoke and
literally means yoking together or union.
Bhagavad-Gita speaks of three paths leading
to the goal of union with the Supreme Spirit:
the karma yoga or union through disinterested
service, bhakti yoga or union through self-
forgetting love and devotion, and jnana yoga
or union through transcendent divine
knowledge. Another yoga, raja yoga, was
later developed by Patanjali in the second
century B.C. Patanjali defined yoga as the
method of restraining the function of mind
from taking various forms. He was the first
sage to systematize the practices of the
yoga, but the practices themselves had been
in vogue in India from time immemorial.

The philosophical presupposition of yoga
is the notion that the human mind by nature
is pure and clean and capable of reflecting
reality. But it became impure by attachment
to the world. Being foreign to the mind, the
impure elements can be removed from the mind
through the practice of spiritual
disciplines. The pure mind is capable of
direct perception, which gives an object the
stamp of reality. The ultimate reality
appears unreal to the impure mind, that is,
the unenlightened, because the reality is not
directly perceived. The needed direct perception can be obtained by spiritual
discipline, which is called yoga. The yoga

aims at enlightening and purifying the mind, so that the mind does its original funciton of direct perception.

The Hindu philosophers observe the four innate tendencies and temperaments in our mind: active, emotional, introspective, and philosophical. Every one's mind has all these temperaments, but one particular trait is predominant, and this predominant temperament indicates to him the appropriate yoga he should pursue.

Some, conscious of their inability to follow the metaphysical and religious disciplines, could take the path of the ritual discipline. The ritual discipline involves a worship of his chosen cult object. However, the objective of this and other two disciplines is the same--to obtain moksha, "liberty" of the real self (atman) from the bondage of the world.

Likewise, the Buddhists had sought and developed the art of seeing into the nature of one's own being. Their spiritual disciplines aim at liberty from all the yokes under which man suffers in this world. For instance, Zen Buddhists[26] had devised their own technicques to lead themselves to satori, "enlightenment." Satori may be defined as an intuitive looking into the nature things in contradistinction to the analytical or logical understanding of them. Practically it means the unfolding of a new world hitherto unperceived in the confusion of a dualistically trained mind. Logically stated, in satori, all the opposites and contradistinctions are united and harmonized into a consistent organic whole. Two famous techniques are mando and koan. The former is a form of rapid question--answer between master and pupil which aims at so speeding the process of thought that it is suddenly transcended. The latter is a word or phrase insoluble by the intellect; it is often a compressed form of mando. Neither has any meaning for the rational mind. These and other techniques have one single purpose: to liberate all the energies properly and naturally stored in each of us, which are in ordinary circumstances cramped and disturbed so that they find no adequate channel for activity, that is, to lead us to satori, or in the sense of Hinduism to moksha.

By way of analyzing these means of salvation which had been expressed among the Orphic Greeks, Hindus, and Buddhists, an attempt was being made to delineate and characterize the main aspects of the circular eschatology. We have seen that the central feature of the circular eschatology is the idea of the path of progress dictated by the law of karma. Through the series of reincarnations or transmigration the progress of life toward the self-realization is being directed according to the law of karma. The individual self of a man in a series of rebirths eventually emerges into the Supreme Self. This final state of life is called moksha, or Nirvana; at this final stage the transmigration or rebirth ceases, and the union between the individual spirit and the unconditioned Brahman or Buddha is consummated.

The circular eschatology streses the point that a man is the shaper of his own destiny and that he is neither bound for an eternal heaven nor a perpetual hell, but makes a continuous journey toward the ultimate goal. It also embraces the idea that the concept of a god is a continuously evolving process in the mind of man.

Notes

Chapter II

1. Gutherie, op. cit., pp. 30ff.

2. Harrison, op. cit., pp. 420, 523, 529.

3. Jane Harrison, Prologomena to the Study of Greek Religion, Chapters 9-12.

4. Harrison, Themis, pp. 14-16; Rose, op. cit., pp. 93-94; Nilsson, op. cit., pp. 216-217.

5. Gutherie, op. cit., pp. 317-321.

6. Ibid, pp. 322-326; Harrison, Prologomena, chs. 9-12; Nilsson, op. cit., pp. 213ff.

7. Frank Thilly-Ledger Wood, A History of Philosophy (New York: Henry Halt and Company, 1955), pp. 80-82; 83-85; 87-89; Raphael Demos, the Philosophy of Plato (New York: Ortagon Books, Inc., 1966), pp. 78ff.

8. Francis M. Cornford, Plato's Cosmology (London: Routledge and Kegan Paul LTD, 1956), pp. 58ff; R.E. Bluck Plato's Life and Thought (Boston: The Beacon Press, 1951), pp. 80-91.

9. I.M. Crombie, An Examination of Plato's Doctrine (New York: The Humanities Press, 1963), pp. 24,ff.

10. R.D. Hicks, Stoic and Epicurean (New York: Russell and Russell, Inc., 1962), pp. 61-65.

11. Ibid., pp. 22-30, 32.

12. R.C. Zaehner, Hinduism (New York: Oxford University Press, 1966), pp. 14 ff; K.M. Sen, Hinduism (Baltimore: Penguin Books, 1961), pp. 45-52.

13. Ibid, pp. 72-77.

14. Franklin Edgerton, The Bhagavad Gita (Cambridge: Harvard University Press, 1974).

15. Zaehner, op, cit., pp. 36-56; Alain Danielou, Hindu Polytheism (New York: Bollingen Foundation, 1964), pp. 232-249.

16. Ibid, pp. 28ff.

17. Zaehner, op, cit., pp. 59-66; 102-107; 125-159.

18. Ibid, pp. 57ff.

19. William H. McNeill/Jean W. Sedlar (ed.), Classical India (New York: Oxford University Press, 1969), pp. 137ff.

20. The Yin and Yang principles are the two cosmic opposites in constant interaction, through which all in the universe are emerged. The events in human society are the results of these two cosmic principles in interaction. The Yin principle is negative side and the Yang principle is positive side, of the cosmos.

21. McNeil/Sedlar, op, cit., pp. 49ff.

22. Zaehner, op. cit., pp. 17-19; 106-111; 147-159.

23. Christmas Humphreys, Buddhism (Baltimore: Penquin Books, 1972), pp. 78ff.

24. Danielou, op. cit., pp. 14ff.; George
    Feuerstein, The Essence of Yoga (New
    York: Grove Press, 1974), pp. 17ff.

25. Ernest Wood, Yoga (Baltimore: Penguin
    Press, 1962); Sir Krishna Press, the Yoga
    of the Bhagavad Gita, (Baltimore; Penguin
    Books, Inc., 1958).

26. D.T. Suzuki, Zen Buddhism, ed. by Wm.
    Barrett (Garden City; Doubleday, 1956),
    pp. 83ff.

Chapter III

The Supernal Eschatology

To some like the ancient Babylonians only the present world-life counts for anything, beyond the present there is no real life. To others like the Hindus, the Buddhists, and the Orphic Greeks the present life on earth is only significant because it provides the spiritual disciplinary environment for the liberation of the hidden real self. To still others the present world-life is only the preparation for the future life, and thus it becomes crucial and determinative for life hereafter in the supernal realm. The ancient Egyptians and the Parsees had followed the last line of belief. They did not look at the present world-life merely in view of the spiritual disciplinary setting for the self-realization. Rather, the present life was seen to continue in the supernal realm. We shall turn to an analysis of the supernal eschatology that had been experienced among the ancient Egyptians and the Parsees or Zoroastrians.

The Ancient Egyptians

From the pre-dynastic period the Egyptians were preoccupied with the prospect of life beyond the grave.[1] They were very much more concerned with what their gods would do to them in the next world than with their province over them in this world. Their preoccupation with the prospect of the future life can be ascertained without much difficulty from various sources of information, ranging from their general atti- dude toward death to the pyramid building and the usage of the words, ba, ka, and abkhu.

57

The general attitude toward death[2] could be visualized by the custom that they used to address letters to dead relatives, and to ask a dead mother to arbitrate between her sons. Articles in the tombs as well as food and drink would have shown the general attitude toward death and the general idea of life hereafter. The other evidences of their deep interest in the future life will be taken up later.

The futuristic orientation in ancient Egypt does not, however, suggest that they neglected the proper care of their relationship with gods for their present well-being. In truth, from the pre-historic period, they had devoted themselves to the matter of well-being.[3] They had assumed that their earthly well-being depended upon generousity of their gods, and they regarded themselves as beneficiaries. From quite early times every family at home had its own divine object. The wealthy families had even chosen someone to attend to their gods and to minister unto their wants. The poor families had often joined together to contribute, according to each one's means, toward a common fund for providing housing for their gods. Thus the gods were an integral part of the family and their destiny was practically locked up with that of the families.

The relationship between the god-benefactor and the man-beneficiary had been long cherished among the early Egyptians.[4] But their prime concern and preoccupation had been with the future life. Perhaps to avouch the point, the so-called solar theory should be noted. An Egyptian hoped, among many other things, that he would sail over the sky in the boat of the sun god Re, in company with the gods of the funeral cycles of Osiris.[5] He thought that this happy journey could be secured for him simply by painting certain pictures of the journey and by saying

over them certain words of power. On a piece
of clean papyrus a boat was to be drawn with
ink, and in it are the figures of gods,
including Isis and Thoth and the deceased.
When this had been done the papyrus must be
fastened to the breast of the deceased; care
was taken that it did not actually touch his
body. Then his spirit would enter into the
boat of the sun god Re each day, and the god
Thoth would take heed of him, and he would
sail off with Re.

This hope seemed to have been promoted as
they weighed in their mind the nature of the
universe.[6] Like others, the Egyptians speculated about the origin and the beginning of
the universe, and as a result, different
hypotheses were drawn up independently in
various centers of culture in the Nile
valley. Among the earliest of these cultural
centers undoubtedly was On, a Lower Egyptian
town near the southern point of the Nile
Delta, which was known to the Greeks as
Heliopolis. The people at On believed that
at the beginning there was nothing but the
primeval ocean, Nun. In it the sun god Atum
created himself. Then from his salvia or
semen he created Shu, god of atmosphere, and
the goddess Teflnet, the consort of Shu. To
this pair were born Geb, the earth god, and
Nut, the goddess of the sky. Geb and Nut in
their turn became the parents of the gods
Osiris and Seth and the goddesses Isis and
Nepthys. Atum and his eight descendants were
adored as the Great Ennead of Heliopolis.

At another center, Khmun or Hermopolis, a
similar theology emerged. Khmun is found
some 180 miles up the Nile from the Delta.
This was the city of the great god That, whom
the Greeks later identified with Hermes,
calling the place Hermopolis. Here
everything began with That, who called into
existence by his word upon the primeval chaos

four divinities: the primeval water, Nun and his consort Naunet; the spatial infinity, Huh and his consort Hauhet; darkness, Kuk and his consort Kauket, and an "obscurity," Amun and his consort Amaunet. These were collectively called the Eight, and this is reflected in the name of their town Khuman, the word for the number eight.

From these two cosmic theogonies it is apparent that the primeval water Nun is the basic principle of the universe. Nun is formless, had no positive feature and of itself assumed no shape. The Egyptians regarded Nun as the basic matter of the universe and all the living things depended upon it. This idea had been the extended thought from the natural phenomena that the ancient Egyptians entirely depended upon the Nile River which had appeared to them to have been flown out of the primeval water. They could not conceive any moment when there was no water, as the Nile existed from the beginning of their settlement, and when man was independent from the water for his living, as they were completely dependent on the gift of the Nile. Consequently, the Nun in their true faith was said to contain the germs of the things which afterward came into existence and constituted the universe itself.

They came to envisage the universe as consisting of a number of spheres, including earth, Geb, heaven, Nut, and the under-world, Dat. The earth, Geb, was conceived as a flat platter with a corrugated rim. The platter floated in the primeval water Nun. The Nun encircled the world forming the outmost boundary. The sky was seen like the vault of heaven, Nut, supported by four posts. Between Nut and Geb was another sphere, called Shu, which stood on earth and carried the weight of Nut. The Nut provided the way along which the boat of the sun god Re made his heavenly course. The underworld, Dat, had its gate at the western section of the heaven, the sun god Re retired in the west and went through the gate of the Dat, and once again was born in the east in the early morning.

One could easily be perplexed and bewildered about the origin of the Egyptian cosmic-theogony. Modern scholarship, however, seems to have provided us with a key to unlock the riddle. It has sought the answer in the Egyptian's general mentality, that is, in the way of thinking of symmetrical balance.[7] Their general way of looking at a thing was characterized by this symmetrical balance. The symmetrical balance in the way of thinking and looking at the universe had been conditioned and enforced by the geographical condition of the land. The Nile River cuts the land almost evenly into two regions. The Nile inundation and retreat annually occurred around the same time, and this annual cycle of the Nile had become a matter of fact to them. The ancient Egyptians had lived on both sides of the Nile valley, and had become aware of the daily cycle of the sun. These seemed to have been the main causal factors for the symmetrical balance mentality. They were gradually being led to the habit of looking at a thing in the symmetrical balance, the part and the counterpart in such a way as the eastern valley of the Nile was counter balanced by the western valley. Evidently they came to regard the universe as consisting of spheres of the part and the counter-part, namely, the four spheres being structured in the scheme of the part-counterpart.

The ancient Egyptians, when they were getting used to thinking in the symmetrical balance, had no difficulty accepting the pharoah's claim of the status of divinity.[8] The gods are one part, and therefore there must be a counterpart, as the Nut is part and

Geb is its counterpart. They had no problem
to ascribe divine attributes to the pharoahs.
They believed that seeing the divine attributes of hu and sia, and maat and ka in two
pairs as one part, their pharoah, the
counterpart, also had the same divine
attributes.

While they had hope for the solar jounrey
in the boat of the sun god Re, they well knew
that they could not do this with the mortal
body which was bound to decay. To hope for
that happy journey then meant to look for a
certain means of preserving the physical body
from its natural decay. In early times the
bodies of the wealthy persons were wrapped in
bandages soaked in natron; otherwise the dead
were simply laid out in wooded coffins or
placed in matlined pits in the sand. But,
remarkeably the warm air and the dry sand,
acting as natural preserving agents, kept the
dead from decaying. Thus the Egyptians acci-
dentally unlocked the secret of preserving
bodies they had sought and from this
experience a variety of ingenious modes of
burial were developed. Their various experi-
ments finally were consummated with the mummification of the dead.

The solar journey in the bark of the sun
god Re had been regarded as a special
blessing. This might not be obtained by
everyone who had hoped for it, however.
Although one might not be able to attain that
special blessing, he had a strong conviction
that his soul after death continued a life in
the tomb similar to the present life,
enjoying the good things of this world and at
times issuing forth in one guise or another
to breathe the air and look upon the fair
land. This was a general conviction,[9] and
this hope was reinforced by the happy sense
of security conveyed by the land itself. The
land of Egypt was quite isolated from other
lands, and this physical isolation produced

this deep sense of security and of special
election. They had come to believe in divine
providence, according to which the land had
been marked off for them from their
neighbors. The physical security of the
land, so different from her neighbors, gave
rise to the assurance that Egypt is the
center of the universe, and to the conviction
that the divine rule could simply come down
to the land of Egypt without any
intermediation.

The ancient Egyptians had begun from the
early historic times to question what part of
man would survive after death. They had a
different view of nature of man from that of
the Babylonians. The ancient Babylonians saw
man as a dichotomy of body and soul, called
napishtu, which they believed disapeared when
man died, becoming a ghost (utukku). On the
other hand, the ancient Egyptians believed
that man was made up of the eight elements:
khat, ka, ba, khu, sekhem, khuibit, ren, and
ab.[10] Khat indicates something in which
decay is inherent, and is simply the physical
body. Ka is something attached to the body,
or a "double" of a man. It is personality or
an abstract individuality. Its characteristic feature is that ka was free to move
from place to place at will. The offerings
made in the tomb were said for the nourish-
ment of the ka. Ba is something like "noble"
or "mighty." It was believed to dwell in ka
and to have the power of becoming corporeal
or incorporeal at will.

Khu stands for the spiritual element, or
man's spirit. It takes a luminous form and
is an intangeble shape of the body. Sekhem
is something like "power." The last three of
the eight elements of man, khuibit, "shadow,"
ren "name," and ab, "heart," are the general
parts of man's identity. Of these eight,
five parts are indestructable: khuibit, ren,
ka, ba, and khu. The last three parts were

63

originally attributed to the supernatural beings, later to the pharoahs, and finally to man. These were individually or collectively the "spirit." When the Egyptians speak of a spirit, they generally meant these three elements.

The spirit, at death, was released from his body. But the Egyptians believed without consistency that the spirit still needed a tangible form in which to dwell. This tangible form was preferably our physical body itself. The reason for their preference was that they regarded the living, the gods, and the dead as the three species of the same gene anthropos. All these three genes were supposed to have the same physical needs, and these needs could best be met in the living body. Therefore, from early times every precaution was taken against the disintegration of the body, and finally they developed the ingenious process of mummification from the Second Dynasty (3100 B.C.).

We have noted that only three parts of man, that is, the "spirit," will survive after death, and that the spirit would still need a tangible physical body to dwell in and depart from at its will. They came to realize, however, that, in spite of their effort to preserve the body through mummification, the body was still subject to deterioration. This problem led them to the alternative, namely, the use of magic power.

The ancient Egyptians were outstanding metal workers. From the earliest period of the working of metals and in their attempt to transmute them, they discovered the magic force. According to the Greek writers, they employed quick silver in the process, whereby they separated precious metals, gold and silver, from native ore. From this process resulted a "black" powder (kamt or gemt) which was

supposed to possess marvellous powers.[11]
Thy concluded that this power in the "black"
powder worked for separating metals from
their ore. Thus, side by side with their
growth of skill in performing the ordinary
process of metal work, there grew the belief
that magical powers resided in fluxes and
alloys. The art of manipulating metals and
the knowledge of the chemistry of metals and
of the magical powers came to be discribed by
the name "khemeia," i.e., the "preparation of
the black ore." To this name the Arabs
affixed the article al, and thus created the
word alkhemeia or alchemy.

In ancient Egypt, two different kinds of
magic were observed, namely, magic which was
employed for legitimate purposes and with the
intent of benefiting either the living or the
dead, and that which was used in the further-
ance of nefarious plots and schemes and
which was intended to bring calamities upon
those against whom it was directed.[12] In
either case, however, the basic objective of
magic was to command the supernal forces to
work for the magicians. This objective was
to be achieved by the use of certain words
which, to be efficient, must be uttered in a
proper tone of voice by a duly qualified man,
a magician. Like the Babylonians, the
ancient Egyptians called upon the magicians
at every turn in their life to ward off the
spirits of the dead, demons, wild beasts,
fire, injury, to protect women in child-birth
and new-born infants, and more diligently to
ensure the dying man happiness beyond the
grave. The magic formulae were often written
on some substance, for example, papyrus, and
almost everyone wore some such charm or
talisman.

Now, being aware of the danger that the
mummy would be still subject to decay, they
could turn to the alternative, i.e., to
magic. There emerged a conviction that, by

means of magical words and proper rites, the
perishable could be changed into the
imperishable. Of all the magical
rites,[13] the most important was that of the
"opening of the mouth and eyes." This rite
was performed either on the mummy itself or
upon a statue which represented it. They
believed that the rite could transmit to the
statue the attributes of the person in whose
image it was made. The words of power were
said to be necessary for anyone to plead for
his innocence in the next world, but without
a mouth it was impossible for him to utter
them. Therefore it was all important to give
him not only the words of power, but also the
ability to utter them correctly and in such a
manner that the gods in the next world would
hearken to them and obey them.

By the time of the New Kingdom (1570
B.C.), the priesthood had produced lengthy
and elaborate books of magical spells, the
"manuals of infernal geography." In this
manual, the dead would find all the questions
they would be asked, and the correct answers
to give. Both noblemen and private citizens
had the scroll of magic placed in their
tombs, or on their mummies. By having done
so, they hoped that this book would look
after their welfare in the next world. One
version of the manual was named "the book of
what is in the Duat" ("under-world"); another
version was called "the book of the gates"
and purported to describe each of the twelve
divisions of the Duat, through which the boat
of the sun god Re passed.

In view of these developments the ancient
Egyptians did not need to worry much about
the decay of the mummy. For by means of the
performance of certain ceremonies and the
recital of certain words of magic power to
the stone statue of the dead, the qualities
and attributes of his soul could be
imparted.[14] By magic power, all the good

things depicted on the walls of the tomb or
coffin were believed to be actually present
when he stood before the final judgment.
Thus, magic was believed to play as large a
part in overcoming the obstacles and meeting
the challenges of the other world as did the
possessor of a spotless record of personal
behavior.

Their belief in magic shows how deeply
pragmatism was embeded in the mind of the
ancient Egyptians. Their pragmatic and practical minds had prevented them from creating
sytematic and uniformed religious outlooks.
In general they simply hoped for the happy
future life and expressed their beliefs in
immortality of the "spirit" in various terms.
The Egyptians of the historical period always
believed in immortality,[15] though there was
no word for immortality in their language.
The same word "life" was used both for
earthly existence and for existence after
death. Modern scholars have discovered that
their early belief in immortality resulted
from the fact that the conditions of the soil
and climate brought about a remarkable preservation of the human body. The perfect
state of preservation which the Egyptians
developed seems to have led them to believe
in life hereafter.[16] But immortality is not
absolute; certain conditions had to be met to
achieve it. Life in the "other land" was a
reward for and conditional upon virtuous and
righteous behavior in earthly life. This
appeared as a competing notion with mere
reliance on the magic power. Stress was
placed on the moral value of a man's action
as a condition of felicity in the other
world. This was shown in the scene of judgement in the hall of Osiris. In the scene,
Osiris is seated on his throne. Before him
are the scales, on which the heart of the
deceased was weighed against the feather of
ma'at, that is, truth and righteousness. The

jackal headed god Anubis watched the tongue of the balance and reported to Thath, the scribe. In case the proceedings went against the deceased, a monster lurked close by, ready to devour him.[17]

The idea of the salvation which is conditional on good works had seemingly been worked primarily on the Osiris cult.[18] Osiris was a passive and a suffering figure. He was totally dependent on the support of his son Horus, and in this way resembled every Egyptian who could imagine his fate after death, through the good service of his son to be, like that of Osiris, a blessed one. All Egyptians were believed to be the sons and children of Osiris as they were related to the god-incarnate, their Pharoah.

Thus, the deeds done on earth were to be subjected to scrutiny before the throne of Osiris. This notion of the final judgment appeared from the early period, but the ancient Egyptians left no information as to the locality where the judgment took place, or whether the soul passed into the judgment hall immediately after death, or after the mummification was ended and the body was deposited in the tomb.

Before the dead person received the final verdict, he had to make his way through a number of regions in the underworld, and to pass through many halls. This journey was made only by the spirit, or soul. The righteous spirit passed from the body and united with the gods in the bliss. The physical body did not rise again, and it was believed never to leave the tomb. Rather, the spirit of the righteous was said to procure another body, which was not a physical body. This new body was totally an otherwordly body, and was believed to be germinated out of the dead physical body. Because of this conviction, the Egyptians

continued to mummify their dead.[19] Most of
the ancient Egyptians put their trust in the
words of Thoth and the prayers of their
priests, which could cause the body to become
changed into a Sahu, or incorruptible, spiritual body, in which the dead dwelled with the
gods.

This notion of immortality, however, had
not been worked out fully from the beginning
of their history. In the Neolithic culture,
there were found in the cemetaries vessels
containing food and drink, tools, arms, and
jewelries. It may indicate a common expectation that the deceased continued in some
form of life in the tomb. But these supplies
to the dead in the grave would not prove that
the Egyptians considered life after death a
mere continuation of life upon earth. They
only show that the Egyptians could not imagine life, in whatever form, to persist while
the requirements of life were superseded.
Life after death was thought to require
sustenance in the form required by all life.
Interestingly enough, the thought that life
after death is sustained by matter led the
Egyptians not to a material interpretation of
life, but to a spiritual view of food. This
was shown by the fact that the offerings at
the tomb were especially made to a man's ka.
This ka implies his vital force and in plural
it means his sustenance.

The general conviction in immortality may
have been reinforced by a popular notion that
the living, the gods, and the dead are the
three species of the same genus, and that
all three are subject to the same physical
needs, to the same habits and desire.
Consequently, the dwelling of all three, the
house of the living, the temple of the gods,
and the tomb of the dead, were constructed on
very much the same pattern. They recognized,
however, the degree of difference; the gods
and the dead occupied the high position.

69

This recognition may have led them to build
the pyramids for the pharoahs and the
notables.[20]

Besides this and the mundane expectation
of a continual life in the tomb, we recognize
a symbolic reason for their use of pyramids.
In a temple at Heliopolis there was found a
symbol called the benben, a pyramid-shaped
stone which represents the sun god Re. Some
suggested that the pyramid itself was an
enlargement of the benben. If this was the
case, the pyramid must have been built to
represent the rays of the sun god Re shining
toward the earth.[21]

During the Hyksos rule the expectation of
a continual life in the tomb seems to have
undergone a substantial modification
toward a new expectation of life in the
supernal realm, where the external and mundane forces could not be allowed to
interfere. About 1720 B.C., an Asiatic
people had invaded and conquered Egypt. The
later Egyptian historian Manetho designated
the invaders "hyksos," which means
"king-shepherds" in the Egyptian language
(hyk, "king" or "prime," and sos,
"shepherd"). The Hyksos had been the
congeries of nations of Syrians, Bedouins, and
Aryans, who moved into the eastern Delta to
pasture their flocks, and were strengthened
later by bands of well-armed tribesmen.
According to Manetho, they established two
dynasties, but had to retire to the east when
Ahmose reasserted the Egyptian rule.

We have already mentioned that the soul
of the righteous passed into sahu or akhu,
that is, the incorruptible, transfigured
spirit. That is to say, the sahu formed the
dwelling place of the soul in heaven just as
the physical body had been its earthly abode.
Their hope for becoming the "trasnfigured
spirits" had often been expressed in more

concrete and visual terms. The transfigured
spirits were seen at night as stars in the
sky, especially in the northern part. They
had neither defect nor suffered diminution
forever. This idea, which emerged after the
Hyksos rule, however, was not totally new.
The word akhu appeared in the inscriptions of
the First Dynasty. But the significant steps
toward the general acceptance of the thought
had been taken primarily due to foreign inva-
sion and rule.

The concept of sahu or akhu suggests the
teleological sphere of the universe, and
now the Egyptians firmly believed that man
would be translated by death from the sphere
of the insignificant to that of the
significant, from an ephemeral and singular
form of existence to one which is lasting and
changeless. The akhu idea, in other words,
indicated participation in the perenial life
of the universe.[21]

We find no inscription in the Egyptian
texts of the plane of bliss such as of the
Elysian Field of the Greeks. The word used
for the dwelling place of the dead is "Reed
Field" or "Field of Rushes," and "Field of
Offerings." The last term seems to suggest
that one must be well equipped to survive at
all. The more usual name, "Field of Rushes,"
refers to the primeval scenery of the Nile
valley. In the pyramid text, the Field of
Rushes was identified with heaven.[22] It did
not have any particular location; it simply
referred to the supernal realm, which was
completely separated and transcendental from
the phenomenal world.

The ancient Egyptians were not interested
in dogmatizing any thoughts and ideas,
including the idea of immortality and the
life after death. To their practical and
pragmatic mind, it was possible to have many
different ideas about their future, each

71

having its own merit and value. One might
hope for joining the sun god Re in his bark
to take the solar journey, acrossing the sky
by day and illuminating the gloom of the
underworld by night. At the same time he
could hope to become one with Osiris or one
of his subjects. One might simply hope for
another life in his tomb, enjoying the good
things of this world and at times coming forth
in one guise or another from the tomb to
breathe the air and look upon the fair land
of Egypt. However, there was, with the
diversity of belief and the hope for the
future, essential unity that man could find
immortality and peace by becoming part of one
of the perennial cyclic rhythms in
the supernal realm. This was believed to
take place parallel to the natural rhythms in
the phenomenal world, like the sun, moon and
the blook of the Nile.

The parsees or the Zoroastrians

By the Parsees or the Zoroastrians, the
supernal eschatology was being articulated.
The parsees are the descendants of the original residents of Pars, an ancient province in
southeastern Iran. Because they preferred
the religion of Zoroaster, they are also
called the Zoroastrians. Prior to them, we
do not find a religious founder in the
ancient Near Eastern pagan world. Unlike the
Hindus, whose religion evolved through the
teaching of a series of prophets, saints, and
sages, without a founder, the Zorastrians
claimed their religion was revelatory through
a single prophet Zoroaster. In distinction
from the Hindus, who do not accept the idea
that a single person has an exclusive mandate
from a god to represent him, the Zoroastrians
believed Zoroaster to be the founder of the
religion and the prophet. This belief became
one of the cardinal doctrines of
Zoroastrianism.

Zoroaster[23] was the son of a priest of a
pastoral tribe. It is not certain when and
where his birth took place. But the
Zoroastrians in general set the date of his
birth at "258 years before Alexander."
Alexander the Great was known to them the
first time when the sack of Persepolis and
the fall of the Achaemenian Dynasty occured
in 330 B.C. Therefore the year 588 B.C.,
arrived at by adding 258 years to the year
330 B.C., would be the year when the prophet
made the initial success of his mission.
This success was believed to have occurred
when he was about 40 years old. From this we
place his birthdate in year 628 B.C. Since
he was said to have lived 77 years, he must
have passed away in year 551 B.C.

According to tradition, when he was born
divine effulgence appeared in the country
proclaiming the divine glory of the prophet.
The tradition goes on to say that the hereti-
cal persons in his home state tried to kill
the infant prophet, but he was miraculously
saved by the protection of the holy spirit.
As a boy he had shown much concern for others
and was deeply interested in finding the
truth of religion. When he was about 20, he
withdrew to a secluded place on the mountain
called Ushidarena, or "the mountain of divine
wisdom." There he spent the next 10 years,
and finally he received the divine message.
Thus at the age of 30 he seemed to have had a
definite spiritual conversion, in which he
believed he encountered an angel, "Good
Thought" (Vohu Manah). The angel apparently
had taken him, through a spiritual trance, to
the Great Spirit Ahura Mazda, "wise Lord,"
who henceforth had become Zoroaster's personal god. This prophetic experience was
followed by many other revelations in the
next decade of his life. As a result, he
felt called to preach a new faith against the
indigenous polytheism in his home country.

73

Zoroaster denounced the polytheistic cultus; he equated the gods with evil spirits, who seduced men from the true worship of the one Spirit. However, he was not monotheist; rather he was monolatrist, who worships one particular god as his favorite deity but recognizes more than one deity, having recognized various personified qualities of the Great Spirit Ahura Mazda, e.g., Amesha Spentas or "Immortal Holy One." Zoroaster is reported to have met persecution as a result of his new faith, and he fled to the ancient Chorasmia when he was about 40 years old. There he begun to proclaim his gospel that eventually resulted in the conversion of king Vishtaspa (Hystaspas), whose rule was overthrown by Cyrus the Great. During the last violent days of the war, a tradition confirms that Zoroaster himself was killed at the age of 77.

Chorasmia is the area now known as the persian Khorasan, or west Afghanistan, and the Turkman Republic of the Soviet Union. In Zoroaster's days the Iranian peoples had fanned out throughout this region. These people included not only the Medes and the persians but also the parthians and the lesser known tribes -- Chorasmians, Soghdians, Bactrians, and many more from farther east. This region had been politically subjected to the constant inroads of many different ethnic groups. Under these circumstances Zoroaster must have come to the conviction that the world was ruled by two opposing forces, good and evil. The good force eventually came to be regarded as a hypostasis of Ahura Mazda, and the evil force as that of a malevolent spirit, Ahriman.[24]

The teaching of Zoroaster was originally written on ox hides, and became the Zoroastrian sacred book, called Avesta,[25] which was said to have consisted of some 12,000 hides. In the course of Alexander the

Great's conques, most of the Avesta was
destroyed, and only a third of it remained in
the memory of men and in the old and late
versions. It is not certain when his
teaching was committed to writing -- perhaps
not before the downfall of the Achaemenian
Empire in 330 B.C. From this time on the
Zoroastrians had the sacred book Avesta.
This was an unique feature of Zoroastrianism.
Before them there were many religious
writings in the pagan world, but no
Scripture. For instance, the Hindus did not
possess a single scripture with a captial S.
The Hindu scriptures were always spelled out
with a small s; by that designation they
expressed the idea that there is nothing
infallible about them.

    Zoroastrianism itself, had passed through
various reforms, and the final results were
mainly in the forms of the "primitive
Zoroastrianism," the "Catholic Zoroastrianism,"
and the "reformed Zoroastrianism." In the
sequel the primitive Zoroastrianism represents the original teaching of the prophet
which has been preserved in Gathas, the
oldest part of the Avesta. The Catholic
Zoroastrianism is a syncretism of the
prophet's message primarily with nature
worship and polytheism, which was the common
heritage of the Iranian and Indian races. In
the Sassanian period, a new dualistic ortho-
doxy became fully developed. In this form,
the wise Lord asserted his absolute ascen-
dency over all creation, though he was now
limited by an independent power, Ahriman,
who, as a separate and co-eternal substance,
could challenge him on his own terms. This
reformed Zoroastrianism, which is a stringent
dualism, finds its most complete expression
in the Pahlavic texts.

    When Zoroaster began to preach his gospel
that the two opposing principles, good and
evil, were at war in the world, he may have

failed to give a definite exposition of the
origin of evil. He was setting forth the
monolatry, and his followers had become the
monolatrists. They worshiped Ahura Mazda,
who was believed to be the creator, the
supreme god, and the most beneficious spirit.
He was also worshiped as absolute good.
Therefore he could not be the author of any
kind of evil, natural or moral. But in the
world, the evil spirit Ahriman acted malevo-
lently in opposition to Ahura Mazda. They
had experienced many evil things in their
ordinary life; their world seemed to be
filled with evil things. It was very natural
for them to begin to speculate on the author
of evil. The origin of evil[26] (sin) had been
one of their long-puzzling questions. Later,
the Zoroastrians seemed to have solved the
problem of the origin of sin and evil, as
they had gradually arrived at more definite
ideas of the history of the world.

According to the late Zoroastrians, the
world had passed through a number of periods,
each consisting of three thousand years.[27]
At the beginning of the first period, Ahura
Mazda produced the spiritual creation.
During this period the spiritual creation
obviously remained in intangible bodies. His
first spritual creation was Vohu Mano, "Good
Mind," in consulation with whom he produced
all others. This period was followed by the
period of material creation of the universe,
and by another three thousand year period.
During the third period a spiritual being,
called Angra Mainyu, broke through its limit
and entered the material creation and thus
casued great distress. Angra Mainyu went
beyond its limit, and thus had become the
author of evil and sin. In this manner, the
Zoroastrians found the way out of the problem
of the origin of sin and evil. It suggests
that they preferred to admit a limitation of
their god Ahura Mazda's power, rather than to
leave room for doubt of his perfect goodness.

76

All the evils in the world were the works of a power hostile to absolute good.

The third period was the age of human history prior to the revelation of the true religion. At the beginning of the forth period, Zoroaster appeared to show the true way of salvation; at the close of the period there would be the final judgment. During this last age, good and evil would struggle against each other, contending against and destroying each other's works. They imagined a time when the perpetual struggle between good and evil would be gradually intensified as the end of the age approached. First, a terrible potentate would appear and nature would be convulsed. There would be a thousand years of appalling strife and bloodshed, in which the angels of Ahura Mazda would take part, and which would end in victory for the forces of good. Another second millennium would follow, during which happiness would be the lot of mankind. During this millennium, however, their faith would grow weak, and the evil one, Angra Mainyu, seeing his opportunity would loose a dragon upon the world. The monster would devour mankind and cause them to commit unspeakable sins, so that Ahura Mazda would be obliged to send the Savior to quell the monster and restore order to the earth. The Savior finally would bring the world to an end and preside over the resurrection and judgment of the dead. The hosts of evil and the wicked would be cast into fire, Hades would finally succumb, and the age of perfect blessedness would begin.

Zoroastrianism did not preach the universal salvation. The Zoroastrians held neither particularism nor predestination, but lay the emphasis on goodness in words, thoughts, and deeds. In creation, man was endowed with a perfect free will, and ever since he maintained that quality, being a responsible

being for his future destiny hereafter.[28]
The word used for free will is daena. In the
Gathas and the late Avesta, the daena is used
in both objective and subjective senses. In
the objective sense, it signifies "religion,"
and in the subjective sense it implies
"conscience," "inner being," and "free will."
By free will or religious conscience was
meant the real determinant of individual
destiny. Sooner or later every human being,
according to the cardinal doctrine of
Zoroastrianism, had to make a free choice
between good and evil or between Truth and
Lie, or between the true religion which the
prophet claimed had been revealed to him, and
the false religion which his contemporaries
had inherited from their forefathers. Those
who had chosen the true religion or the Truth
were the righteous. In the teaching of the
prophet, however, the righteous originally
meant the peaceful pastoral population which
was constantly threatened in the eastern
Iranian provinces by the nomadic tribes.
Zoroaster referred to them as the "followers
of Truth."

In a sense, man's perfect free will was a
kind of hypostasis of intelligence and
goodness, through whom Ahura Mazda had created
the world. Thus Ahura Mazda had become imma-
nant in the world. One of Ahura Mazdah's
attributes, Vohu Mano, "Good Mind," was not a
mere metaphysical conjunctive between the
unchanging and changing world of becoming,
but an immanance and an embodiment in the
universe. In other words, an embodiment of
"good mind" in man was free will. The "good
mind" worked as a free will and the specific
guardian. That is to say, Ahura Mazda, the
hypostasis of "good mind," was believed to be
condescended to the mind of mankind. He
could do this by virture of having a number
of divine attributes. Some of them were
regarded to be inseparable from his essence,
namely, the Holy Spirit, the Good Mind,

Truth, the Wholeness, and the Immortality.
But the attribute of Right-mindedness was
regarded to be in common to both Ahura Mazda
and mankind and to represent a right relation
between the two.

Right-mindedness was to cooperate with
free will in man, but without confusion,
compulsion, or conflict. Each individual had
his own mandate to run the course of his own
free will. When he chose to follow the
course of Truth, Right-mindedness became an
additional fiat to his free will.

Man, being endowed with free will, was a
responsible being and the arbiter of his own
destiny. He, however, could not avoid taking
part in the struggle between good and evil,
since mankind was divided, according to its
own free choice, into the good, upright and
pious, and the evil and atheistic. The
former follows Ahuru Mazda, and the latter
Ahriman. The good life was meant to be an
unceasing struggle against evil within and
without. Virtue, like purity, was seen as a
defeat of evils; therefore morality had a
streneous and militant quality.

By fidelity to Truth was meant the
virtuous life that had to be shown in the
triad of good thoughts, good words, and good
deeds. This triad constituted the
Zoroastrian ethics, and this system of penances assumed the meaning of expiation. The
commonest of these penances was horse-
whipping from as few as five stripes up to
ten thousand. The flagellation was supposed
to drive out evil. The purpose of this and
other penances was expiation for delinquency
in life in respect to the triad.

In a more practical sense, to choose the
side of Truth was meant to give hearing to
the prophet, who was believed to have given
to mankind a full message of hope for the

future. His prophetic mission was to reveal
the message. However, what had come to him
was not how Ahura Mazda was to be praised or
worshipped, but what the god would have man
believe and how he would have him live.
Faith and good work thus had become two
imperatives and prerequisites of salvation.
However, in distinction from other pagan
religions, magic played a very minor role in
Zoroastrianism. Rather, it commended a high
virtue and morality, and the moral character
superceded the magical efficacy which was
most highly valued among the ancient
Egyptians. The moral character lay not in
overt actions alone, but in the inner spring
of conduct.

When Ahura Mazda created man, he
gave him physical, mental, and spiritual
powers. Man's responsibility was to cultivate and utilize those powers in the service
of Ahura Mazda and of humanity. The primary
tenet was to keep himself in physical,
metnal, and spiritual purity and to lead an
honest and simple life of virtue, devotion,
faith, industry, and benevolence. The
Zoroastrians held the notion in common that
there could be a healthy mind only in a
healthy body, and that without physical
health a man could not perform the duties in
life. Man was believed to fulfil three kind
of duties in life, namely, to Ahura Mazda, to
himself, and to others.[29] In pursuance of
these duties, the Zoroastrians were
instructed to follow the threefold "pathway
to the god." First, they should seek unity
and harmony in any apparent diversity, acting
as a mediator among men. Second, they should
lead a life of utter self-abnegation, being
not only selfless but also charitable.
Thirdly, they should foster freedom of
conscience.

They were not only commanded to follow
the "pathway to the god," but also to be

faithful with "three great obligations."
They were obliged to dedicate all the abili-
ties to Ahura Mazda, to accept Zoroaster to
be the true guide of spiritual matter in order
to resist all the temptations and hardships,
and to rely absolutely on divine dispensation,
never doubting the decrees of their god.

The emphasis was laid equally upon repentance and expiation. The old teaching of
Zoroaster in the Gathas knew nothing of
renunciation and sin. But the Pahlavi texts
speak of two kinds of renunciation and sin.
One was a secular offense which involved an
injury done to a person or an animal and must
be satisfied by an act of atonement. The
other was internal sin which affected only
one's own soul and could be sufficiently
atoned for by performing, or causing others
to perform, good works. Both sins were to be
confessed to the priests, and the forgiveness
of the sins depended largely upon the
person's determination to avoid such offenses
in the future. It should be noticed that the
Zoroastrian expiation consisted in performing
acts of merit so as to heap up a store of
good works. Only in this way could their sin
be completely remitted. The offences which
thus confessed and properly expiated were
canceled and were not to be accounted for at
the final judgment.

It is worthy to note that the eschatological issues, including the final judgment,
were not definitely spelled out in the
Gathas. But the late Avesta mentioned
briefly that the soul of the dead hovered
near its earthly tenement for three days and
three nights before it passed to the final
judgment. This thought was elaborated in the
Pahlavic and other later texts. When the
righteous passed away, his soul took its seat
near the head, chanting the sacred hymns and
proclaiming the happiness which Ahura Mazda
would accord to the blessed. At daybreak on

81

the fourth day, a perfumed breeze came to him
from the south and with it came a beautiful
maiden daena ("conscience"). Now, the soul
of the righteous passed into the "endless
light," into the company of good and into the
presence of Ahura Mazda.

According to a different version, the
good angels conducted the soul to the Cinvat
bridge, protecting it from any assault of
demons on the way.[30] Mithra, Sraosha, and
Rashna sat in judgment. Rashna weighted a
man's merits and demerits in the true
balance. The Zoroastrian profession of good
faith and the penitent confession of sins
weighed heavily on the side of salvation.
For the good, the Cinvat bridge is wide, and
he passed with ease to the heavenly mansions
on the other side. The wicked found it
narrow as a razor-blade, and pitched headlong
into the gulf below. He eventually arrived
in the "infinite darkness," and until the
resurrection his soul must be in this hell,
in much misery and torment of many kinds.

When the appointed time came, all the
dead would be raised, and all assembled in
one place. We should note the meaning of
the Zoroastrian resurrection. Here the
resurrection (frasekereti) implied rehabili-
tation which was described as "ageless,
immortal, undecaying, not-rotting,
ever-living, ever-prospering, and
self-sufficient" (yast 19, 11). After the
general resurrection of the righteous and the
wicked, the former were ushered into the
"best existence." In later Persian language
"best existence" became known as bihest,
"paradise." The "best existence" also
received different designations: "house of
praise," "house of treasure," and "house of
reward." All these designations characterize
the final state of the righteous as being the
best of praise and thanksgiving, and
receiving abundant reward and blessing from

Ahura Mazda. On the other hand, the wicked would be cast into the eternal hell, "infinite darkness."

With this, the world finally completed its fourth and final period, and all these escha-tological events took place in the supernal upper realm.

Notes

Chapter III

1. Walter B. Emery, Archaic Egypt
   (Baltimore: Penguin Books, 1969), pp.
   119ff; Pierre Montet, Eternal Egypt (New
   York: American Library, 1968), pp. 167ff.

2. Adolf Erman (ed.), The Ancient Egyptians
   (New York: Harper Torchbooks, 1966), pp.
   8ff.

3. George Steindorff and Keith C. Seele,
   When Egypt Ruled the East (Chicago: The
   University of Chicago Press, 1957), pp.
   132-137.

4. Henri Frankfert, Ancient Egyptian
   Religion (New York: Harper Torchbooks,
   1961), pp. 14ff.

5. Erman, op. cit., pp. 138-146.

6. Kramer, op. cit., pp. 130-134; Frankfort,
   et al., op. cit., pp. 51ff.

7. Ibid., pp. 47-50.

8. Steindorff/Seele, op. cit., pp. 82ff;
   Kramer, op. cit., pp. 34ff; Frankfort,
   op. cit., pp. 49-58.

9. Frankfort, et al, op cit., pp. 39-42.

10. Frankfort, op. cit., pp. 96ff.

11. Sir, E.A. Wallis Budge, Egyptian Magic
    (London: Routhledge and Kegan Paul,
    1972), pp. 19-21.

12. Ibid., pp. 304.

13. Ibid., pp. 182ff.

14. Ibid., pp. 17ff.

15. Steindorff/Seele, op. cit., pp. 144ff.

16. James Henry Breasted, The Down of
    Conscience (Chicago: The University of
    Chicago Press, 1933), pp. 49-50; 272ff.

17. E.F. Statcliffe, The Old Testament and
    the Future Life, p. 7.

18. Budge, op. cit., pp. 41ff.

19. Budge, Egyptian Ideas of the Future Life,
    1899, p. 170.

20. The Theban Kings of the South did not
    engage a pyramid construction. Instead,
    they built underground temples for
    themselves.

21. The name for pyramid, M(e)R, implies
    the place of ascension, and some of the
    early pyramid texts refer to the pyramids
    as "a staircase to heaven" and "a place of
    ascension."

22. The region represents some district of
    the Delta. We have a picture of it in
    the papyrus of Nebseni (British Museum
    No. 9900), the oldest on papyrus and from
    this "the Field of Reeds" (sekhet-aaru)
    typified some very fertile region. Cf.
    Frankfort, op. cit., pp. 111-113.

23. R.C. Zaehner, The Dawn and Twilight of
    Zoroastrianism (New York: E.P. Putnam's
    Sons, 1961), pp. 33ff.

24. Hendrickus Berkhof, Christ, The Meaning
    of History (Richmond: John Knox Press,
    1962), p. 19; A.V.W. Jackson, Zoroastrian
    Studies (New York: Amo Press Inc. 1965),
    pp. 28-35.

25. Zachner, The Dawn, pp. 25-26.

26. Another way of solving problem of the
    origin of evil and sin was worked out,
    and this was known as Zurvanism. According
    to this school, both Ahura Mazda and
    Angra Mainyu issued from a first prin-
    ciple known as Zurvan Akarana, "Infinite
    Time," which is beyond good and evil.
    Both were brought into sturggle from the
    temporal World. The temporal World
    itself contained the seed of evil, as
    well as good. Only within this order is
    the contrast meaningful. But the supreme
    Being dwells in a glorious eternal state,
    beyond these conflicts and contrasts. Cf,
    Miles M. Dawson, The Ethical Religion of
    Zoronster (New York: Amo Press, 1969),
    pp. 94-98.

27. Jackson, op, cit., pp. 110-115.

28. Ibid., pp. 132-142; Zachner, op. cit.,
    pp. 265 ff.

29. Dawson, op. cit., pp. 114 ff.

30. Jackson, op. cit., pp. 145-151.

Chapter IV

The Historic-linear Eschatology

The Judeo-Christians

The Linear Time Concept

In the previous discussion, we noted that the non-Judeo-Christians in general conceived the world as moving aimlessly in a circle. Their history revolved around a universal center of life and destiny, called "universal soul, or logos, or atman."[1] Time was moving in an endless circular course in which every thing keeps recurring. In this perspective they saw an ultimate end of human life. The ultimate end of human life is a transference or liberation (moksha) from an existence bound in this world in the circular course of time into Beyond which absolutely retired from time into timeless infinite.[2]

They could not find in history any significant patterns and movements moving toward a definite goal; simply a meaningless succession of events made up history. Having thus conceived of history, the ancient Babylonians, who were pantheistic existentialists, had to find a way from nonauthentic to authentic existence by making an acceptable decision to their given society alone. This social imperative, which the political, socio-economic and other cultural elements in their society demanded, pessimistically created the historic-terminal eschatology which was marked by a philosophy of the absolute mundane primacy in their lives.

The ancient Greeks also had very little, if any, sense of history as moving toward a definite end. Such a concept did not suit the Greek mind. They sought for perfection, which in reality meant "static harmony." The ancient Greeks could not expect to find it in changing events in the circular course of time. All changing events are finite, and any finite had as such no abiding meaning. At their best, they could say that the eternal absolute is reflected in their history, sometimes more, sometimes less, but always in a broken and distorted form.[3] The historic finites occur in endlessly repeated cycles, so that what is happening today will some day be repeated. Consequently, the ancient Greeks were unable to conceive of history as moving toward a definite goal.[4]

This non-Judeo-Christian concept of history is totally foreign both to the ancient Hebrews and the early Christians. The unique feature of the Judeo-Christian idea of history, as it is revealed in the Bible, is the fact that human history has been moving steadily on an upward sloping line with a "beginning" (arche) and toward an "end" (telos). The "end," to which our history is moving, is not a timeless beyond but an endless-time, "eternity." At the "end," the present age takes a new order of affairs of eternity in a new heaven and a new earth. This upward sloping line is divided into two time divisions at the advent of Jesus Christ.[5]

This two divisions of history are variously called: this world and the world to come, this time and the world to come, this present time and the world to come, this world and that world, and the present age and the age to come.[6] These appellations set the two ages in a radical contrast and in an antithesis. This antithesis, between the present age and the age to come, does not, however, suggest that times and eternity are placed as opposites. Nor does it imply that the "present age" is time while the "age to come" is timeless. The antithesis between the

two ages simply resulted in the beginning of
the present age when man had fallen into sin.
Thus, the Fall of man into sin became the
determinative of the antithesis. We do not,
however, suggest that the Fall of man created
the time category itself, but that it
involved in the power of evil the course of
events which fill the present age, while the
course of events which fill the age to come
is marked by the conquest of the evil powers.

This radical contrast between the two
ages has teleological character. Human
history has an ultimate end, toward which the
present age moves on. In history, the one
eternal, living God is working out His own
sovereign purpose, the central feature of
which is the sending of His messiah to the
world (Gen. 3:15) for the good of His creation, first for His chosen people, and through
them for the rest of mankind. The Judeo-
Christians saw history as the work of a personal divine will, contending with the stub-
born will of men, promising and warning,
judging and punishing, yet sifting, saving
and aboundantly blessing those found amenable
to discipline and instruction. Through all
this long struggle, the divine purpose of
creating His chosen people is painfully and
patiently wrought out. The purpose of
establishing His chosen people, Israel, was
to fulfil His promise made to Abraham: "In
thee shall all families of the earth be
blessed" (Gen. 12:3).[7] Even at the darkest
hour, when human pride and self-will seem to
have completely frustrated the divine program,
the divine promise still stands, and through
all the visissitudes and changes of human
history, the purpose of God executes toward
its ultimate goal.

In reality, the divine purpose was and is
being carried out through the three stages:
before the creation of the present age,
between creation and the coming of the

Messiah, and after the advent. The first stage before creation was concerned with the whole divine council in which God had already chosen His own, and the plan of their redemption and the last detail of the destiny of the Gentiles were already designed.[8] The second stage is the present age between creation and the coming of the Messiah. At the beginning of the present age the messianic promise stood: "I will put enmity between thee (a tempter) and the woman, and between thy seed and her seed, it shall bruise thy head, and thou shalt bruise his heel" (Gen. 3:15). This promise was made to Adam, and he, as the head of the human race, received it. Thus the promise was universalistic. In the revelation of this promise, God restricted Himself to His chosen people, Israel, due to the growing spread of godlessness and lapse of the nations into heathenism. God carries out His promise, during this stage, the present age, first through and in His chosen people, and then in and through "the seed of Abraham" par excellence, Jesus Christ (Gen. 3:16), whom at "the fulness of time" He sent to this world.

In the unfolding of the divine purpose, the third stage begins with the coming of the Messiah. For Christians, this is the second advent of Christ, but for the ancient Hebrews the coming of Christ is undivided between the first and the second advents. The era after the coming of Christ partakes of the new order of affairs in eternity.

Here we ought to note that in the Bible "eternity" does not suggest the Platonic or modern philosophical sense. It is to be thought of not as something different from time but as endless time, incomprehensible to men. The Greek word aion for our word eternity designates both an exactly defined period of time and an undefined and incalculable duration.[9] While another Greek word kairos has to do with a definite point of time which has a fixed content,[10] the word aion has to do with a duration of time.

The Judeo-Christians always understood time realistically, that is to say, in terms of what happens in it. Here we simply mean that time for them was not a mere chronological continuum but a theological-teleological series. They made a contrast between "realistic time" (kairos) and "chronological time" (chronos). The importance of this distinction lies in the fact of God's control over history as distinct from nature (the material universe).[11] The present age consists both of the "realistic time" and the "chronological time," and both were the means of which God makes use in order to reveal His redemptive purpose.[12]

The "realistic time" after the coming of Christ, that is, in the third stage (= the age to come) in the unfolding of the divine purpose, becomes aion or olam in Hebrew, "undefined- endless time." Olam or aion sometime took on a spatial meaning and so came to mean "world" or "universe."[13] The present age thus eventually comes to an end at the moment when the age to come moves on a higher level. There is a tension, however, between the present age and the age to come as the powers of the latter have errupted into the present age. This tension is a natural consequence of the first advent of Christ, in whom all events of the two ages are summed up.[14] Therefore the Messiah was regarded as a "midpoint" of history.[15] This implies that Christ is the center of history, not in the sense of "universal soul or logos," but in the sense of lordship. Christ is the Lord over all (Matt. 28:18; Phil. 2:9 ff.).

The early Christians used a short form of the public confession, Kyrios Christos. This confession expressed their faith of Christ's universal Lordship. Under the Lordship of Christ the present age is moving toward the ultimate end, to the state of consummation of the divine purpose. The age to come thus was comprehended as the age of consummation and the final realization of the promise made to Adam (Gen. 3:15) and to Abraham and to his descendants (Gen. 12:1-3). The present age is a vehicle, so to speak, whereby God, not man, realizes His purpose in creation with man and the universe. Thus the Judeo-Christians saw history as the working out of God's eternal plan.

The present age has two distinct phases of "the last or latter days" and "the last day." In the Old Testament, "the latter days" means "later times or later days." The latter days come "in the uttermost part of the days" of the Messianic age (Gen. 49:1; Num. 24:14; Isa. 2:2-4; Micah 4:1-8). In the New Testament, "the latter days" includes the entire Messianic age, i.e. the present age between the two advents of Christ (2 Tim. 3:1-5; Acts 2:16, 17; Heb. 9:26; James 5:3; 1 Cor. 10:11; 2 Cor. 6:2; 1 Pet. 1:20; 4:7).[17] The latter days anticipates "the last day" to arrive toward the end of the Messianic age. The last day is certainly the last day of "the later times," and between the latter days and the last day no contrast was made. Rather, the progression of time between the two is only observable. The early Christians were conscious of being in the latter days. Because of the progression of the latter days without contrast or interruption toward the last day, they did not take pains to separate their present being in the latter days from their future presence in the last day (2 Tim. 3:1; 1 Pet. 1:5, 17, 20; 2:1-10; Jn. 7:37; 13:1; Heb. 1:2).

According to the supernal eschatology, the present age is divided into two realms: the realm of spirit, light and good god, and the

realm of matter, darkness and evil god. But
in view of Judeo-Christians, the present
world (age) is not evil. Even though it is
plagued with evils and the domain of Satan,
it in itself is good. God not only created
it but also sustains it. He clothes the
lilies of the field and feeds the ravens, and
is even concerned for the sparrows, one of
the most insignificant birds (Lk. 12:4-7, 22
ff.). He makes the sun to rise on the evil
and good and sends rain upon the just and
unjust (Matt. 5:45). He is the Lord of
heaven and earth (Lk. 10:21). Nothing in
cretion is morally bad. In our moral
dimension, for instance, to achieve
everything one could desire on the human
level is not evil, but it does not minister
to a man's true life which can be found only
in relation to God. Of course, when the
riches of the world became the chief end of
man's interest so that they crowded out the
things of God, they become an instrument of
sin and death (Lk. 12:16-21, 30; Mark 10:27).

In the Old Testament, the prophets saw
the opposing forces in the world not only as
adversaries but even more as an instrument of
God's rule (Isa. 10). But their knoweldge
that God struggles in history with his adversaries, the enemies of His people, did not
lead Israel to the pagan dualism of a good
god and an evil god in conflict, and of the
kingdom of good and the kingdom of evil.
Rather, the Judeo-Christians firmly believed
that God is sovereign over His own struggles
(Ps. 24, 46, 47, 48), and that He even uses
the adversaries to execute His judgment or to
chastise His people (Ps. 75, 93). The fall
of ancient Israel and the destruction of the
Jerusalem Temple in the year 70 A.D. do not
mean victory for the adversaries, but rather
chastening by God's loving wrath, aided by
His adversaries (Isa. 24-27; 45:15; Ezek.
36-39; Dan. 7). He intervenes in the
historical events and turns them into a
"guided history," and leads them to a goal.[16]

The Coming of Christ: Advent

The present age moves toward this final goal, and the ultimate goal is to be found at the time of the second coming of Christ. Just as the Bible prophesied the first advent of Christ, even so in many places it prophesied His second advent.[18]

In the New Testament, a number of terms in connection with His second advent are employed in order to show the nature, manner, and purpose of the advent. The word which occurs more frequetly than any others is parousia.[19] The word parousia was used with the ordinary sense to suggest "presence" (2 Cor. 10:10; Phil. 2:12), as well as "arrival." When it was used for the advent, it never meant "presence." Parousia expresses these aspects of the advent: its public, visible character, its suddenness, and its catastrophic eventuation as opposed to a series of successive events. His parousia will be visible; just as His followers were literally able to see Him ascending into heaven, even so will men be able to see Him descending from heaven.

Christ Himself told His disciples that when He comes again men would see Him "coming on the clouds of heaven, with power and great glory" (Matt. 24:30; Rev. 1:7).[20] The coming on the clouds of heaven speaks poignantly of the nature of the parousia. These words do not mean to localize the event of the parousia. "The clouds of heaven" is more than a mere terrestrial phenomena. Sometimes, the clouds, as in the case of Christ's ascension, is what covers and conceals (Acts 1:9; Rev. 11:12). On the other hand, in the Old Testament, it often suggested God's glory and presence among the people (e.g. Ps. 97: 2 f.; Exod. 13: 20-22; 24:15-18). As to His return on the clouds of heaven, the emphasis was laid on the actuality of His coming and His being seen in glory and splendor.[21]

His parousia will also be sudden. He
said: "As the lightening cometh out of the
east, and shineth even unto the west, so
shall also the coming of the Son of man be"
(Matt. 24:27). The catastrophic aspect of
His return was noted in these words: "In
such an hour as ye think not, the Son of man
cometh" (Matt. 24:44), and "like a thief in
the night the day of the Lord would come" (1
Th. 5:2).

The word apocalypse, "revelation," is
another term used for the advent of Christ (2
Th. 1:7; 1 Cor. 1:7; 3:13; 1 Pet. 1:7, 13;
4:13). The flavor attaching to this word
differs from that carried by the word
parousia. The latter chiefly concerns with
believers, while the former enemies of His
people, though in neither case exclusively
so. The Apostle Paul told this to the
Thessalonians: "Seeing it is a righteous
thing with God to recompense tribulation to
them that trouble you; And to you who are
troubled rest with us, when the Lord Jesus
shall be revealed from heaven with his mighty
angels: (1 Th. 1:6, 7). For believers His
apocalypse will partake of the character of a
"revelation," inasmuch as His glory has not
been fully disclosed to them before. To
unbelievers it is the militant revelation
rendering vengeance. His apocalypse will
bear the feature of a strikingly momentary,
miraculous act; it is a direct translation
from the heavenly sphere into the earthly
region.[22]

Christ's second coming is also called
epiphaneia, "manifestation" (2 Th. 2:8; 1
Tim. 6:14; 2 Tim. 4:1, 8; Titus 2:13). Like
the word parousia, the epiphaneia charac-
terizes His return in glory and power.

In several places, His return is named
"the day" (Mark 13:32; 2 Cor. 3:13; 1 Th.
5:4), "the day of the Lord" (1 Th. 5:2; 2 Th.

2:2; 1 Cor. 5:5), "the day of the Lord Jesus" (2 Cor. 1:14), "the day of Jesus Christ" (Phil. 1:5), and "the day of Christ" (Phil. 1:10; 2:16). In the Old Testament, the Day of the Lord was closely associated with nature-change. The Prophet Amos noted that on the day of the Lord strange things will happen to nature: "And it shall come to pass in that day, said the Lord God, that I will cause the sun to go down at noon, and I will darken the earth in the clear day" (8:9).[23] The day of the Lord is also called "the day of visitation" (Isa. 10:3; Jer. 46:21; 48:44), "the day of wrath, trouble, and destruction" (Jer. 2:27; Zeph. 1:15; Ob. 12). These words seem to suggest that the day of the Lord to the enemies of His people is the day of judgment.

The prophets also saw the coming of the day of the Lord in which He will be the center of the entire scene of battle and victory (Amos 5:18; Isa. 9:4; 49:8; 51:4-6; 52:1-6; 66:10-24; Hos. 1:4b). They associated the day of the Lord with "light," as opposed to the darkness which pertains to the night, and looked forward to the coming of the day of the Lord. For "the remnant," that is, a true Israel, there was coming the day of the Lord, a day of deliverance, joy and blessedness.[24] On the day of the Lord, God will vindicate His people and He begins His eternal reign (Isa. 2:17, 18; 40:9, 10). On that day He will also transform the material universe and inaugurate a new order of the new heaven and new earth (Isa. 35:1; 65:17; Hos. 2:9; Jer. 33:16).

In speaking of His second coming as the day of the Lord, Jesus should have had in view these Old Testament prophecies. He told to the members of the Sanhedrin, when He was being questioned, that today you can challenge my messiaship, but "the day" will come and "ye shall see the Son of man sitting

on the right hand of power, and coming in the
clouds of heaven" (Mark 14:62). On other
occasions, in speaking of the day of the
Lord, Jesus again placed Himself in the third
person, "the Son of man."

In the Gospel, we find two categories of
Jesus' sayings about the Son of man: those
in which He used the title with reference to
the eschtological work He must fulfil in the
future, and those in which He applied it to
His earthly ministry. The eschatologicl work
of the Son of man on the day of the Lord is
that of judgement (Matt. 25:31-46; Mark 8:38;
Jn. 5:27; 6:39-54; 12:48). Jesus, the Son of
man, will come again to carry out the final
judgment. In the Old Testament, Daniel
already prophesied this and said:

> I saw in the night visions, and behold,
> one like the Son of man came with the
> clouds of heaven, and came to the Ancient
> of days, and they brought him near before
> him.
> And there was given him dominion, and
> glory, and a kingdom, that all people,
> nations, and languages, should serve him;
> his dominion is an everlasting
> dominion... (7: 13, 14)

Jesus could call Himself the Son of man
during His earthly ministry, although He did
not come to earth "on the clouds of heaven,"
because He as the Son of man will judge the
world on the premise of His redemptive work,
which was accomplished on the cross. We must
note that, while the title of the Son of man
coming "on the clouds of heaven" is associated with the final judgment, the earthly
Son of man is related to His humiliation and
unites itself with the suffering of the
Servant of God (Mark 10:45; Matt. 20:28).
Thus in the title of the Son of man, the
meaning of the cross and the glory of
Christ's parousia are epitomized. In other

words, His cross sets the eschatological process which will culminate at the triumph of
the Son of man over the enemies of His people
and the establishment of a new order of
affairs on the day of the Lord (cf. Rev.
16:14-16).

To convey this eventuality, the new
Testament writers used another designation of
the second coming of Christ, namely, telos,
"end."[25] God Himself called that "I am the
beginning and the end" (Rev. 21:6), that is,
the eternal one, who brought all things into
being, will make all things new in the eternal order. The early Christians entreated
for His coming by saying Maran-atha, "the
Lord cometh." Surely the second coming of
Christ had become the blessed hope of
believers throughout the ages (Titus 2:13;
James 5:8; Heb. 9:28; 1 Pet. 5:4; 2 Pet.
3:10; 1 Jn. 2:28); on that day all things of
the present world will come to their end.

Some scholars alleged that
Jesus and also St. Paul taught the imminent
advent in their own generation.[26] This is,
however, quite contrary to His own admission
that He did not know the hour of His return
(Mark 13:32). Other saying of His,
therefore, cannot be understood as indi-
cating the date of His advent.[27] Some of His
sayings leave room for the passage of a con-
siderable amount of time before His
advent.[28] St. Paul indicated even in his
early ministry that some, including himself,
may die before His advent (1 Th. 5: 9-10).[29]
He also, in speaking of Christ's second
coming, used a figure of a thief (1 Th. 5:
2-4); the meaning of this figure was well
known among early Christians. The figure
stood for the uncertainty of time of the
advent and the need for constant readiness
for the advent (2 Pet. 3:10; Rev. 3:3;
16:15).[30]

63742

The Signs of the Time

Although Jesus did not reveal to His people the date of His advent, He had taught them various signs of the times for the sake of their being "watchful" for His coming (Rev. 16:15; Matt. 24:42-44, 45-51; 25:1-12). When His disciples "came unto him privately, saying, Tell us, ...what shall be the sign of thy coming, and of the end of the world" (Matt. 24:3), He engaged the Olivet Discourse (Matt. 24) with them to show the signs of His return and of the end-time. From the Olivet Discourse it is clear that "the signs of times" point to what God had done in the past (cf. Matt. 16:3), and also point forward to the advent and the end of history. In the former instance, the signs reveal that God is at work in the world, fulfiling His promises and bringing them to the final consummation of redemption. In the latter case, the signs of times assure believers that the advent will take place on the basis of what God had already done in the past.[31] While God, by the signs of the times pointing to the past, continues to summon men to believe in His Son Jesus Christ and be saved, He also, by the same signs of the times pointing forward to the advent, calls for constant watchfulness.[32] We, therefore, must not think of the signs of the times as referring exclusively to the end of history and as if they had to do only with "the last day."

1. The sign of the preaching of the Gospel to all nations.

In the Olivet Discourse, Jesus said: "And this gospel of the kingdom shall be preached in all the world for a witness unto all nations; and then shall the end come" (Matt. 24:14). The Hebrew prophets anticipated this sign. Habakkuk said: "For the earth shall be filled with the knowledge of

101

the glory of the Lord, as the waters cover the sea" (2:14).[34]

The objective basis of the sign of proclamation of the Gospel to all nations is Christ's death and resurrection, and this objective foundation is God's gracious intervention into human history. This sign, first of all, points backward to this objective basis on which the offer of the Gospel can now be made. On the same objective basis, Jesus had given to early Christians the great Commission: "Go ye therefore, and teach all nations, baptizing them in the name of Father, and of the Son, and of the Holy Ghost" (Matt. 28:19). Thus the sign of the preaching of the Gospel and the Great Commission are inseparably associated. In obedience to His command, the Christian church must preach the Gospel throughout the world as "a witness to all nations." Here "all nations" does not mean that every last individual be converted before the advent and the end of the present age, nor that every person must hear the Gospel before the advent.[35] Rather, it means that wherever the Gospel is being proclaimed, it becomes a force to be reckoned with by the nations. The preaching of the Gospel simply gives to the present age its primary meaning and purpose.[36]

According to some among modern scholars, this sign does not refer to a preaching of the Gospel in our time, or near the end of the present age, but to a preaching that was to occur before the destruction of Jerusalem and its temple in the year A.D. 70.[37] This opinion, however, does not do justice to the main subject in the Olivet Discourse, namely, the disciples' request of the signs of the second coming of Christ and of the end of the world. In the Markan parallel to the Matthean passage (24:14), it says: "And the Gospel must first be published among all

102

nations" (13:10). In both passages "first" in Mark and "then" in Matthew show the clear chronological determination: "first" or "then shall the end of the world comes." In these Gospels and also in the Lukan Gospel (Lk 21:7-19; 20-24), the proclamation of the Gospel is named as a sign along with the eschatological "woes": wars, famines, and pestilence.[38]

The preaching of the Gospel as a sign is revealed to the Apostle John in the figure of the first horseman (Rev. 6:1-8). There in a vision John saw the four apocalyptic horsemen. The description of the first horseman has nothing in common with the ominous appearance of the other three, inasmuch as the sign of the proclamation of the Gospel in the synoptic Gospel has nothing in common with the other signs of war, famine and pestilence. The first horseman is rather a luminous figure. He rides a white horse; in the Book of Revelation, the white color appears as a heavenly attribute. The crown with which he is adorned gives to him the character of a beneficient power. John said that he went out as a conquerer and to conquer. In the book of Revelation, "conquerer" does not have the meaning of violence; on the contrary, it designates divine action. In Rev. 19:11 ff., the rider on the white horse is called "faithful and true." This same name "faithful and true" also implies the word of God (Rev. 1:5, 3:14). In the light of these and other passages (e.g. Zech. 1:8; 6:3, 6), our understanding is that the first horseman has the task of preaching the Gospel to the world. The other three horsemen signify the signs of the end, and like them, the first horseman is a sign of the end. Here the implication is that, as a last offer of salvation, the proclamation of the Gospel to all nations runs parallel to all those terrors which are symbolically depicted in the

103

other three horsemen. The necessity for repentance to be preached before the end is stressed in other places in the book of Revelation (11:3; 14:6 f.; cf. Acts 1:6 f.).

The Apostle Paul implied the sign of the preaching of the Gospel in these words: "And now ye know what withholdeth (restrains) that he (the man of lawlessness) might be revealed in his time" (2 Th. 2:6). Here the Greek word for "to restrain" (katechein) has a temporal meaning in the sense of "retard" or "delay." The question before the Thessalonian Christians was when will Christ come? St. Paul gave his answer in these words: "Let no man deceive you by any means: for that day shall not come, except there come a falling away first, and that man of sin (lawlessness) be revealed, the son of perdition" (2 Th. 2:3). St. Paul went on to say that the man of lawlessness has been restrained that he might be revealed in his time. The man of lawlessness is said to come "only he who now letteth ("restraints") will let, until he be taken out of the way" (2 Th. 2:7). Here St. Paul meant that the "restraint" is the preaching of the Gospel to all nations and that the man of lawlessness comes after the preaching to the Gentiles, just as he will come after that which "still restrains."[39]

2. The signs of wars, famine, earthquake, and persecution, and of the great tribulation

In the Olivet Discourse (Matt. 24, Mark 13; Lk. 21), wars, conflicts, earthquake, and persecution even to the point of death were regarded as preliminary evils, and these characterize the "beginning of woes." There are some similarities between the Olivet Discourse and Rev. 6 in content as well as structure: a time of preliminary troubles marked by evils in human society and in

104

nature, followed by a short time of great tribulation.[40]   In the light of Rev. 6, which deals with the woes which will come on "the great day" of the Lord (v.17), we would not say that these preleminary evils refer to the evils which occur only before the destruction of Jerusalem in the year A.D. 70.

A short time of great tribulation which follows the period of these preliminary evils is also known as "the time of Jacob's trouble." The prophet Jeremiah said: "Alas! for that day is great, so that none is like it; it is even the time of Jacob's trouble; but he shall be saved out of it" (30:7). Daniel also saw the coming of great tribulation and said: "There shall be a time of trouble, such as never was since there was a nation even to that same time" (12:1). These words are echoed in the Olivet Discourse: "For then shall be great tribulation, such as was not since the beginning of the world to this time, no, nor even shall be" (Matt. 24:21).

These words were the prophecy of the destruction of Jerusalem which occurred in the year A.D. 70 and of great tribulation which the fall of Jerusalem brought upon Israel. Some, therefore, argued that Jesus was not speaking of the so-called great tribulation toward His second coming. The last sentence in our Matthean quotation, "no, nor even shall be," suggests that the greatest tribulation of all time was to occur at the siege of Jerusalem by the Romans. They went on to say: "It would have been pointless to have added that comment if it was to occur at the end of the age, for then of course no time would have been left for such an occurrence."[42]   Against this opinion, one might hasten to point out that the method Jesus used in the Olivet Discourse was a "prophetic foreshortening," in which events far removed in time and events in the near

105

future are spoken of as if they were very
close together.

We once more remind ourselves of the
question placed before Jesus Christ in the
Olivet Discourse. The question was when will
the destruction of Jerusalem occur? His
answer was related to the two events - immediate event and distant-eschatological event.
The immediate event was the fulfilment of the
prophecy of Daniel 9:24-27 which was concerned with the end of the Old Testament
Jewish worship and opening up the good news,
the New Covenant, to all without discrimina-
tion (v. 27). This prophecy was to be
fulfiled through the destruction of
Jerusalem. The distant event was the
fulfilment of Daniel's extended prophecy,
namely, the end of the present age, which is
preceded by the great tribulation, and this
was typified by the destruction of Jerusalem.

Jesus placed these two events into the
closest approximation and had shown to His
disciples the signs of the times of these two
events. He chose to describe the signs of
the times in terms of the people of Israel
who were to come to their end as the chosen
people, and were to face the great tribulation in the very near future. The greatest
tribulation of all time at the siege of
Jerusalem by the Romans was to be a type of
the great tribulation which will come upon
believers toward the end of the present age,
that is, in "the last day." His words, "no,
nor even shall be," marked the finality or
the end of the nation of Israel as a chosen
people, and the finality or the end of the
present age. Thus, these words "no, nor even
shall be," have a dual reference, namely, in
reference to the end of the Jewish nation as
a chosen people, a beginning of the new
dispensation and of "the latter days," and in
reference to the finality or the end of the
present age, arrival of the age to come.

We could say this because Jesus also
indicated that this great tribulation will
immediately precede His second coming in
these words:

Immediately after the tribulation of
these days shall be the sun be darkened,
and the moon shall not give her light and
the stars shall fall from heaven, and the
powers of the heaven shall be shaken; and
then shall appear the sign of the Son of
man in heaven: and then shall all the
tribes of the earth mourn, and they shall
see the Son of man coming in the clouds
of heaven with power and great glory
(Matt. 24:29, 30).

These apocalyptic and symbolic words were
also found in the prophetic announcements about
God's judgment against Babylon: "For the
stars of heaven and the constellations
thereof shall not give their light: the sun
shall be darkened in his going forth, and the
moon shall not cause her light to shine"
(Isa. 34:4, 5). These words were also pro-
nouned against Egypt (Ezek. 32:7, 8). In
these prophetic announcements, some scholars
have found an analogy, and applied the same
apocalyptic words in the Olivet Discourse to
the destruction of Jerusalem alone. As these
apocalyptic words in the prophecies pronounced God's judgment against the pagan
nations, so the same apocalyptic words in the
Olivet Discourse pronounced His judgment
against Israel. God carried out His judgment
against Israel through the destruction of
Jerusalem.[43]

This analogy, however, was not based on a
solid foundation. Since in one respect
Christ's advent was related to the final
judgment, the prophetic apocalyptic language
was quite fitting for St. Matthew who was
dealing with the significance of the advent.
St. Matthew would have been encouraged to use

these apocalyptic words by Joel who said:
"The sun shall be turned unto darkness, and
the moon into blood, before the great and the
terrible day of the Lord come" (2:31, cf.
2:10). Here Joel prophesied that in the day
of the Lord, when God will finally visit the
earth in both judgment and redemption, the
entire earthly order will be shaken. The
apostle John also saw cataclysmic phenomena
in nature which signaled the coming of the
day of the Lord Jesus Christ (Rev. 6:12-17).

Even when we applied these apocalyptic
words to the destruction of Jerusalem alone,
which was God's final judgment against the
unfaithful Israel, there still remains an
analogy between God's judgment against Israel
through the destruction of Jerusalem which
came toward the end of the history of Israel,
and God's judgment on the day of the Lord
against all nations toward the end of the
present age.

Those who regarded the great tribulation
as having occurred already at the time of the
destruction of Jerusalem in the year A.D. 70,
appealed for support to these words in the
Olivet Discourse: "Verily I say unto you,
this generation shall not pass, till all
these things be fulfilled" (Matt. 24:34).
"This generation" here was taken as referring
to a people living at the time when Jesus
said these words.[44] However, "this
generation" has a temporal sense and also a
qualitative sense. In the temporal sense, it
means the generation of people living at the
time when Jesus spoke these words. In this
case "all these things" include the advent,
and also implies that Jesus was setting a
date of His second coming. This violates His
disavowal that even the Son of man does not
know the date of His parousia. In the qualitative sense, "this generation" means either
the Jewish people or unblievers from the time
when Jesus spoke these words until His second

108

coming. In this case, "all these things" means the destruction of Jerusalem and the sufferings which will accompany the destruction, and which is a type of the end of the world.[45] "All these things," in a sense, means the signs of the end exclusive of the parousia itself, and people who were living while Jesus was speaking these words will see all these precursory signs of His second coming without seeing the coming itself.[46]

The great tribulation will not be basically different from earlier tribulations, which Christians have had to suffer, but will be an intensified form of those earlier tribulations.[47] In reality, tribulations are the opposition of the world to the kingdom of God. Because of the continual opposition of the world to the kingdom of God, Christians must expect to suffer tribulations during the present age. There will be a final, great tribulation just before the second coming of Christ. Woes and cataclysmic phenomena to the universe are associated with His return.

Sufferings and tribulations basically occur in Christian lives because all the results of sin have not yet been eliminated.[48] The complete elimination of the consequences of our sin will only be realized at the time of Christ's return. Therefore St. Peter said to his readers: "Beloved, think it not strange concerning the fiery trial which is to try you, as though some strange thing happened unto you: But rejoice inasmuch as ye are partakers of Christ's sufferings; that, when his glory shall be revealed, ye may be glad also with exceeding joy" (1 Pet. 4:12-13). St. Paul also told the Colossians that the affliction Christ had to suffer will continue in His church (Col. 1:24). In fact, the Christian church represents her Lord to the world

through suffering, and suffering is a vital
part of the fellowship with Christ.
Suffering is the lot of the church,[49] and
this follows from the fact that suffering was
central in the life of Christ. Jesus
forewarned at the outset of His ministry:
"Think not that I am come to send peace on
earth: I came not to send peace but a sword"
(Matt. 10:34). Jesus here meant that the
suffering will be an unavoidable and recogni-
zable indication of the presence of His reign
on earth. This was why it was often spoken
of in great soberness and in an undertone of
deep joy (e.g. Matt. 5:10; Acts 5:41; 1 Th.
3:2; James 1:2).

Christians enter the kingdom of God
through many sufferings and tribulations
(Acts 14:22), and their present sufferings
are tied with their future glory (Rom.
8:17-18). They are to suffer "until the
completion of the number; yet those who
suffer and die for Christ will receive the
white robe of victory" (Rev. 6:9-11; 21:4).
Thus the New Testament represents tribulation
as the lot of all true believers, and it is
so "great," intensively as well as
extensively, as to refer to the entire period
of the present age.

What we just said is contrary to the view
that the great tribulation is the wrath of
God poured out upon an apostate world. The
great tribulation and the wrath of God are
not the same, however. Believers will not
suffer His wrath. They are delivered through
the blood of Christ forever from His wrath (1
Th. 1:10; Eph. 5:6). God's wrath is revealed
from heaven against all unrighteousness and
ungodliness of men (Rom. 1:18). The wrath of
God is resting only on the one who refuses to
believe in Christ (Jn. 3:36; Rom. 2:5; Eph.
2:3; 5:6).

110

3. The sign of apostasy

Among early Christians, in particular among the Thessalonian Christians, some thought that the day of the Lord was in the process of approaching really now to them. Consequently, they had given up working and were living in idleness. This led St. Paul to correct them, and he wrote these words: "Now we beseech you, brethren, by any means: for that day shall not come, except there come a falling away first, and that man of sin (lawlessness) be revealed, the son of perdition" (2 Th. 2:3).

The article before "apostasia" (apostasy) and the statement that this happening must precede the second coming of Christ indicate that the apostasy here predicted is a final one just before the end of the present age, and a culmination of a falling away from faith or a general apostasy which had already begun way back in history. A general apostasy was already happening even in St. Paul's time. The Apostle Paul wrote to Timothy: "In the latter times some shall depart from the faith, giving heed to seducing spirits, and doctrines of devils; speaking lies in hypocrisy; having their conscience seared with a hot iron" (1 Tim. 4:1, 2). This general apostasy goes along with moral decadence. Hence St. Paul pointed out to Timothy the presence in these "latter days" of "lovers of their own selves, covetous, boaster, proud, blasphemers, disobedient to parents, unthankful, unholy..." (2 Tim. 3:1 ff.).

Apostasy, according to St. Paul's words, is "falling away from the faith." On the other hand, St. Paul taught us that the true believers are "the purchased possession" (Eph. 1:14), that is, God's own inheritance. Unless God Himself disowned them, the true believers will not fall away from their faith

(Jn. 10:27-29; 1 Pet. 1:3-5). It is then
clear that apostasy is outwardly associated
with the people of God (1 Th. 2:18, 19; 1 Jn.
2:18, 19). Christ linked, in His Olivet
Discourse (Matt. 24), apostasy with the
appearance of the false prophet (24:4-5,
12).[50] In essence, apostasy is unbelief that
is lived, while the true faith has to be
lived.

4. The sign of "the man of lawlessness" or Antichrist

   In the New Testament, because "the man of
lawlessness" and "antichrist" are very similarly described, the early Christian church
applied the designation, antichrist, to that
of "the man of lawlessness." The distinctive
feature of Antichrist or the man of
lawlessness is the denial of the deity of
Christ, and this denial strides at the entire
fabric of man's salvation. Here the preposi-
tion "anti" expresses the sense of
"opposition," and an antichrist is the
irreligious, anti-religious, and anti-
messianic par excellence.

   In our Thessalonian passage, "apostasy"
and "the man of lawlessness" or Antichrist are
conjoined by the conjunction "and." This
suggets that Antichrist will arise out of the
apostasy, and that the latter itself will
culminate by the appearance of Antichrist.[51]
The Apostle John also spoke of the same truth
in these words: "Little children, it is the
last time: and as ye have heard that
antichrist shall come, even now are there
many antichrists ..." (1 Jn. 2:18). Here St.
John made a temporal distinction between
antichrists who were present and Antichrist
who shall come in the future. In other
places, he said that Antichrist was coming in
the false teachers (1 Jn. 4:1; 2 Jn. 7).
Since Antichrist was already manifested in the
false teachers, he also said that it is "the

last hour" (1 Jn. 2:18) to characterize contemporary time as eschatologically meaningful
and to call his readers to watchfulness in
the face of the danger of the false
teachings. When we ordinarily say this is
the last hour, we also have the same warning
to be exceptionally watchful.

The Apostle John also made a "reality"
distinction between an antichrist as a person
and antichrists as anti-christ tendencies and
powers which were to be consummated in a personal figure, Antichrist (1 Jn. 2:22; 4:3).
St. Paul's language, "the man of lawlessness"
or "the son of perdition" and his statement
about the man of lawlessness (2 Th. 2:3-12)
confirm this reality distinction. Jesus
spoke of Judas as "the son of perdition" (Jn.
17:12). The prefix "son" or "man" marks a
person as the supreme manifestation or expo-
nent of the quality spoken of. Inasmuch as
Judas, "the son of perdition," was a human
being, "the man of lawlessness" or "the son
of perdition," spoken of by St. Paul, is also
a human person. Here we should also point
out that an antichrist in 1 Jn. 2:22 was
thought of as a person, since the definite
article was used with the word. Antichrist,
however, stands out as far removed from the
purely naturalistically human, because St.
Paul said: "Even him, whose coming is after
the working of Satan with all power and signs
and lying wonders" (2 Th. 2:9).

Several attempts have been made to identify Antichrist with a historic or non-
historic figure. Some identified Antichrist
with Belial. The Apostle Paul referred to
Belial when he spoke of the temple of the
living God (2 Cor. 2:14-18). In the Old
Testament, nowhere does Belial (Beliar)
appear as a name directly given to a person,
but it is always given in the company of pre-
fixes for the purpose of attaching to the
person or thing referred to an evil

connotation: e.g., "certain men, the
children of Belial" (Judges 20:13); "a
daughter of Belial" (1 Sam. 1:16); "sons of
Belial" (1 Sam. 2:12). We are not yet certain about its derivation. Belial, etymologically considered, may suggest
rebelliousness, lawlessness, degradation, or
worthlessness.[52] The LXX translators favored
the rendering of "lawlessness" (e.g. Deut.
5:9; 13:13; 2 Sam. 22:5; Ps. 18:4). In Nahum
1:11 Belial was used in the personal sense,
but in 1:15, it was used as the description
of a person, "wicked one."[53]

In the book of Jubilees, one of the
Jewish apocalyptic books, those Israelites
who disobeyed their ordinance of circumcision
were called sons of Belial (15:33). Belial
was also regarded as deceiver (Jub. 1:20) and
oppressor (T. Benja. 3:3). Belial was
placed, in opposition to their God, in the
position of prince of darkness (T. Lev. 19:1;
T. Joseph 20:2; T. Zebu. 9:8), and in close
connection with fornnication (T. Sim. 5:3; T.
Issa. 6:1). These passages thus show that
Belial is of wickedness and an adversary, but
we are not assured if Belial passed as a
technical name for Antichrist. The Sibylline
Oracles distinguished Belial from Sabaste or
Satan (3:63). But in other places Belial was
described as descending from the firmament,
having his habitation in the air and being
the chief of the powers of the world; in all
these passages Belial in character is identified with Satan.[54] On the other hand,
Belial was spoken of in the context of the
ethical exhortation to the Israelites, as St.
Paul referred to Belial in the same ethical
context, namely, righteousness and iniquity
and light and darkness can have no more in
common with each other than Christ can have
with Belial (2 Cor. 6:14-16).[55]

St. Paul's own words, "he ("the man of
lawlessness") as God sitteth in the temple of

God" (2 Th. 2:4) and "the mystery of iniquity doeth already work" (2:7) seem, according to many commentators, to indicate that St. Paul was writing of a person and an event of his day, not of the remote future. Accordingly, the apostasy was meant the Jewish apostasy, which would reach its climax at the time of the destruction of Jerusalem and the dispersal of the Jewish people, and the man of lawlessness or Antichrist was meant a Roman emperor, or the line of the emperors of the first Christian era. According to this interpretation, "he who now letteth (restrains) will let, until he be taken out of the way" (2 Th. 2:7 b) was meant the Jewish state, under whose protection for a short period of time the early Christian church should grow strongly enough to withstand all difficulties.[56] In fact, Judaism enjoyed freedom of worship, being a legalized religion, when early Christianity was born in the Roman Empire. It was quite possible for early Christians to have received the same privilege with their contemporary Jews when the Romans could not make a clear distinction between Judaism and Christianity.

This interpretation faced, however, a grammatical difficulty in our text. As we already pointed out, in 2 Th. 2:3, "the apostasy" and "the man of lawlessness" are closely conjointed by "and," and this suggests that both complement each other. If the apostasy is the Jewish apostasy, then the man of lawlessness must be found in the Jewish apostasy.

St. Paul undoubtedly had in view the prophecy of Daniel in a vision of four beasts. In the vision, Daniel saw "a little horn" coming up which had "eyes like the eyes of man, and a mouth speaking great things." (7:8). This little horn was taken by many commentators to represent "a small kingdom whose power is concentrated in its king, here

represented by the eyes and mouth."[57]   In
order to guard against the little horn being
considered as possessing more than human
character, Daniel used the description of the
eyes of man.   This little horn was but a man
and was generally identified with Antiochus
IV Eiphanes, king of the Seleucide kingdom
(175-163 B.C.).[58]   In Daniel's passage pride
and self-exaltation, haughtiness,
contemptuousness, usurpation, radical
opposition, and blasphemy (11:36 ff.) are the
main personal traits of the little horn.
Before the little horn there came the ten
horns which represented a later phase of the
fourth beast or kingdom.   Historically
the symbolic fourth beast stands for the
Roman Empire, and to the Roman Empire the ten
horns or kingdoms traced their origin, though
not immediately, to Rome.

From the time of the fall of the Roman
Empire[59] to the appearance of the little horn,
there would have been ten kingdoms which
truly partake of the character of the fourth
beast, namely, the Roman empire.   The number
ten here might be taken as the symbol of
completeness.   Thus Daniel's prophecy implies
that the appearance of the little horn will
occur at the end-time ("the last day"), and
Antiochus IV Epiphanes was a type of this
eschatological figure which will partake of
the personal character and the sacrilegious
conduct of Antiochas IV Epiphanes.

Also, an attempt had been made to identify "the man of lawlessness" or Antichrist
with a Roman emperor, Nero.   Nero, the arch-
persecutor of Christians, was believed to
return from his death in 68 A.D., and then,
with the help of Satan, through supernatural
influence and activities, set up a new phase
of his wicked reign, and conduct with an
antichristian persecution.

This Nero redivivus theory was worked out from the form of cryptogram used by St. John in Rev. 13:18: "Here is wisdom, Let him that hath understanding count the number of the Beast; for it is the number of a man; and his number is six hundred threescore and six." The number 666 here meant to refer to Nero (Neron Kaisar). Neron Kaisar first was transplanted into Hebrew, which has total 666. But there still needed a slight variation in the spelling of the Hebrew word for Caesar.[60] In Rev. 13:1, 2, 5 and 17:3, 7-12, the seven heads and ten horns are identified by many commentators with the first seven Roman emperors and ten kingdoms,Nero held the fifth place. Under the sixth emperor these verses were written, and, according to Nero redivivus theory, these verses embodied the expectation that after a brief reign of his next two successors Nero will return from the death to assume the role of Antichrist.[61]

From the analysis of Daniel 11:36-45, a different identification of the man of lawlessness or Antichrist was made. In verses 1-35, Daniel prophesied the divisions of the empire of Alexander the Great and the wars between the kings of the Seleucide and Ptolemid kingdoms in the north and in the south respectively for dominion over the Holy Land. Antiochus IV Epiphanes was shown to be type of Antichrist (21-35). The prophecy of Antiochus IV Epiphanes leads up to the revelation of Antichrist in verses 36-45. The verse 36 says: "And the king shall do according to his will; and he shall exalt himself, and magnify himself above every god, and shall speak marvellous things against the God of gods, and shall prosper till the indignation be accomplished: for that that is determined shall be done." This verse has a parallel in 2 Th. 2:4, which was regarded as the correct interpretation of Daniel's passage (11:36). Daniel's next verse 37 gives an additional description of

117

Antichrist: "Neither shall he regard the God of his fathers, nor the desire of women, nor regard any god: for he shall magnify himself above all." This verse has a Jewish emphasis and has reference to the Jewish religion. Here the king is said to have not regard for the God of his fathers and, in a sense, he has no regard for the Jewish religion. The one who has no regard for the Jewish religion, obviously is himself a Jew, and he is Antichrist.

This conclusion that Antichrist is a Jew, and he will arise from among those who outwardly were associated with the Jewish religion was reinforced in our Thessalonian passage, 2 Th. 2:3 ff. We already stressed the point that the apostasy and the man of lawlessness are conjoined by the conjunction "and." The apostasy, "a falling away from faith," here will occur among the people who acknowledge the true God. The title "the man of lawlessness" signifies the aggravated sinfulness to the degree of denying Christ and exalting himself above God Himself. Both St. Paul and St. John meant Antichrist the supreme embodiment of the spirit of unbelief with regard to the true Christian Gospel as centered in the messiahship of Jesus. Both the apostasy and the man of lawlessness stand for the Satanic corruption and prostitution of the Jewish messianic hope and of the Christian hope for the second coming of Christ.[62]

According to Daniel 11:45, Antichrist will make his last stand in territory which is sacred and holy, and will come to his end (cf. Zech. 14).[63] We found St. Paul's comment on this prophecy in these words: "And then shall that wicked be revealed, whom the Lord shall consume with the spirit of his mouth, and shall destroy with the brightness of his coming" (2 Th. 2:8). The prophet Isaiah similarily prophesied the end of

Antichrist and said that the Lord shall slay
the wicked with the breath of His lips
(11:4). According to the Apostle John's
testimony, there will be a battle in a place
called Armageddon, and in the course of the
battle, Antichrist will come to his end (Rev.
16:12-16). The only weapon invovled in this
warfare is the word of Christ ("the spirit of
his mouth," "a sharp sword").[64] This indicates that the battle of Armageddon is not of
the warfare between the spirits of good and
evil. Rather, this warfare is an instrument
which God designed in bringing His just
judgment upon Antichrist and his followers.
Finally, Antichrist, which is also called
"the beast" (the first beast) in the book of
Revelation will be "cast alive into a lake of
fire burning with brimstone" (Rev. 19:20).

Until this happens to Antichrist, and,
during the entire present age, "the
restraining hand" is present to ensure that
Antichrist or the man of lawlessness shall be
revealed only at the proper time (2 Th. 2:6).
The proper time is God's own time and not
Antichrist's. God is almighty and rules all;
He is all in all (1 Cor. 15:28). He hindered
the final outburst of lawlessness to proceed
from Antichrist, though He lets "the mystery
of iniquity" (lawlessness) to work for the
present until "the restraint" ceased to
act.[65] Thus until the time of the parousia
the closing catastrophe will be averted.

<u>An Overview of the Signs of the Times</u>[66]

I. The Signs of the Times of "the last
   days" (the present age)

   A. The general signs:
      1. Wars
      2. Famines
      3. Earthquakes

119

4. Pestilences
5. The proclamation of the gospel to all nations
6. The moral decadence

B. The typical (types) signs:
   1. False prophets
   2. "Falling away from faith" (Apostasy)
   3. Antichrists
   4. "The little horn" = Antiochus IV Epiphanes
   5. The fall of Jerusalem in 70 A.D.
   6. Tribulations and suffering

II. The Signs of the Times of "the last day" (the end-time):

A. The apostasy
B. The false prophet (the second beast)
C. Antichrist (the man of lawlessness, the son of perdition, the little horn, the beast)
D. The great tribulation
E. The woes of the seals (Rev. 6:3-8)

Notes

Chapter IV

1. B. C. Bentan (ed.), The Idea of History
   in the Ancient Near East (New Haven: Yale
   University Press, 1955), p. 39.

2. O. Cullmann, Christ and Time
   (Philadelphia: The Westminster Press,
   1949), pp. 52-53; E. Jennis, "Time," IDB,
   R-Z, p. 648.

3. Berkhof, op. cit., p. 20.

4. John Massh, The Fulness of Time (London:
   Nisbet, 1950), p. 167; Cullmann, op.
   cit., p. 52; Berkhof, op. cit., pp. 19-21
   Karl Lowith, Meaning in History (Chicago:
   The University of Chicago Press, 1949),
   pp. 405; Antony Hoekema, The Bible and
   the Future (Grand Rapids: William B.
   Eerdmans Publishing Company, 1979), p.
   24.

5. Once the Stoics held that there were four
   "ages of the world" and that each of the
   recurrent circles of time may be divided
   into four parts, each part being called
   an "age." Cf. C. R. Smith, the Bible
   Doctrine of the Hereafter, p. 103; Plato,
   Timaeus, 37d; Aristotle, Physica, ed.
   W.D. Ross, Vol. 11, Book IV, 219a.

6. E.g. Matt. 12:32; 24:3; Mark 10:30; Lk. 18:30; 20:34, 35; Rom. 12:2; Eph. 1:21.

7. Cf. Exod. 19:6; Isa.61:6; 1 Pet. 2:5, 9; Rev. 1:6; 5:9, 10; 20:6; James Orr, The Problem of the Old Testament, pp. 37-38.

8. See Eph. 1:4; 3:8ff.; Jn. 1:1ff.; Col. 1:16ff.; Cullmann, op. cit., pp. 52-53.

9. Ibid., pp. 45-46.

10. E. g. Acts 1:7; 24:25; 1 Th. 5:1ff.; 2 Th. 2:6; 1 Tim. 2:6; 6:14; 1 Pet. 1:11; Titus 1:3; Rev. 1:3; 11:18.

11. John Marsh, Fulness of Time (London; Nisbet, 1952), pp. 54-55; 287.

12. In addition to kairos and chronos, in the New Testament, "now," "today" and "hour" also were used to express the idea of special point of time, at which point God will bring about His purpose, e.g. Heb. 3:7, 13; Col. 1:26.

13. The word olam came to be used for "time" past and "days of old" (Isa. 63:9; Mica 5:2; Jer. 5:15; Ps. 24:7; 93:2). It can be used of the remote time in definite future. In this case, it means "for ever," whether it refers to the life time of the individual, or to the perpetual duration of the earth (Ecclesia 1:4) or sky (Ps. 68:6). Also, it is used as a title for God, e.g. El Olam (Gen. 2:33), In this case, the idea is rather moral than metaphysical, and reference to His covenant relationship with Israel (2 Sam. 7:26; 2 Ch. 33:7; Exod. 3:14).

14. See Col. 1:16-20; Geerhardus Vos, The Pauline Eschatology (Grand Rapids: Wm. B. Eerdmans Publishing Co., 1961), pp. 17-18. Cf. 4 Ezr. 7:50; Sir. 18:10; Apoc. Bar. 48:7; 61:15.

15. Cullmann, op, cit., p. 72.

16. Berkhof, op. cit., p. 21.

17. Edward J. Young, My Servants the Prophets (Grand Rapids: Wm. B. Eerdmans Publishing Co., 1955), p. 68.

18. E. g. Isa. 59:20; Jer. 23:5; Dan. 7:13; Zech. 14:4; Job 19:25; 1 Th. 4:16-17; 2 Th. 1:7-10 (cf. Zech. 14:5; Isa. 2:10; 49:3; 66:15; Jer. 10:25); 2 Th. 2:4 (cf. Dan. 7:27; 8:23-25; 11:30-40); 1 Cor. 3:13-15 (cf. Zech. 13:9; Mal. 3:3; Jer. 17:10; Isa. 8:22).

19. E.g. I Cor. 15:23; 1 Th. 4:15; Matt. 24:3, 27, 37-40; Titus 2:13.

20. All the Scripture quotations are made from Authorized King James version.

21. G. C. Berkouwer, The Return of Christ (Grand Rapids: Wm. B. Eerdmans Publishing Co., 1972), p. 164.

22. Vos, op. cit., p. 79.

23. See Amos 6:7; Isa. 13:9f.; Ezek. 32:7 f.; Joel 2:10 f.; Zeph. 1:14-16.

24. E. g. Hos. 2:18; Isa. 10:20; 52:6; Jer. 30:8; Ezek.29:21; Sibyl. Orac. 3:796 ff.; Enoch 37-71; Apoc. Bar. 72: 2 ff.

25. Matt. 24:3, 6, 14; 1 Cor. 1:8; 15:24; 2 Cor. 1: 13, 14; 1 Pet. 4:7; Heb. 3:6, 14; 6:11.

26. Among those who advocated this and Christ's own error, on the basis of the study of Matt. 10:23; Mark 9:1; Lk. 9:27; Matt. 16:28 are: Albert Schweitzer, The Quest of the Historical Jesus (London: A. and C. Black, 1954); F. Buri, Die Bedeutung des N.T. Eschatologie für die neuer Protestantische Theologie (Zurich, 1935); M. Werner, The Formation of Christian Dogma (Naperville: Allenson, 1957); O. Cullmann, op. cit.; W.G. Kummel, Promise and Fulfilment (Naperville: Allenson, 1957); C. H. Dodd, New Testament Studies (Manchester: Manchester University Press).

27. Cf. Hoekema, op. cit., p. 113; N. Stonehouse, The Witness of Matthew and Mark to Christ (Philadelphia; The Presbyterian Guardian, 1944), p. 240; F.F. Bruce, New Testament History (Garden City: Doubleday and Co., 1972), p. 197; H.N. Ridderbos, The Coming of the Kingdom (Philadelphia: Prebyterian and Reformed, 1962), pp. 503-507.

28. Matt. 24:14; 25:14-30; Mark 13:7; 14:7, 9, 43-44; Lk. 12:41-38; 19:11-27.

29. H.N. Ridderbos, Paul: An Outline of his Theology (Grand Rapids: Wm. B. Eerdmans, 1975), pp. 490-492; Berkouwer, op. cit., pp. 92-93; Hoekema, op. cit., p. 125.

30. Paul Minear, Christian Hope and the Second Coming (Philadelphia: Westminster Press, 1954), pp. 135-136.

31. Ridderbos, Paul, pp. 522-523.

32. Hoekema, op. cit., p. 135.

33. Berkouwer, op. cit., pp. 238, 244-246.

34. See Joel 2:28; Isa. 40:5; 45:22; 52:10.

35. Hoekema, op. cit., p. 138.

36. Ridderbos, The Coming of the Kingdom, p. 382.

37. This is the Postmillennial interpretation; see Loraine Boettner, The Millennium (Grand Rapids: Baker, 1958), p. 192; J.M. Kik, The Eschatology of Victory (Philadelphia; Presbyterian and Reformed, 1971), pp. 98 ff.

38. These woes also were to occur before the destruction of Jerusalem according to the Postmilennialism.

39. The rabbinic answer to a question of who is delaying the coming of the man of lawlessness is "the still unfulfiled repentance of Israel, and this answer tends toward the Christian view of the eschatological necessity of the preaching of the Gospel to the Gentiles. Cf. Cullmann, op. cit., pp. 164-166; Mal. 3:1; Sir. 48:10, 11; 1 En. 47:4, 4 Ezr. 4:35f.

40. George E. Ladd, A Commentary on the Revelation of John (Grand Rapids: Wm. B. Eerdmans, 1976), p. 98.

41. Beottner, op. cit., p. 192; Kik, op. cit.

42. Boettner, op. cit., p. 191; Kik, op. cit., pp. 98 ff.

43. E.g. Kik, op. cit., pp. 32-35.

44. Boettner, op. cit., pp. 194-195.

45. Calvin, Harmony of the Evangelists III,
    151-152; Ridderbos, The Coming of the
    Kingdom, pp. 500-503; Hoekema, op. cit.,
    pp. 116f.

46. Ladd, The Presence of the Future (New
    York: Harper and Row, 1964), pp. 320-321;
    cf. Cullmann, Salvation in History (New
    York: Harper and Row, 1967), pp. 214-215;
    Werner Kummel, Promise and Fulfilment
    (Naperville: Allenson, 1957), pp. 59-61.

47. Wm. Hendrikson, The Bible on the Life
    Hereafter (Grand Rapids: Baker, 1959), p.
    127.

48. Cf. Acts 14:22; Rom. 5:2, 3; 8:35; 12:12;
    2 Cor. 1:4; 2:4; Eph. 3:13; 1 Th. 3:4; 2
    Th. 1:4.

49. See Jn. 16:33; Acts 14:22; Heb. 12:5-11;
    2 Th. 1:4; 1 Pet. 4:12; Rev. 1:9; 2:9,
    10.

50. Cf. Eph. 4:13f; Gal. 3:1; 1 Tim. 1:19; 2
    Tim, 2:18; Heb. 6:5; 10:26; 2 Pet. 2:20;
    Rom. 11:11; 1 Cor. 10:12; Rev. 2:5; Jn.
    3:19.

51. Hoekema, op. cit., p. 154.

52. Three possibilities are:
    1. be - li, "without" plus ol, "yoke"----
       Belial suggesting rebelliousness,
       lawlessness, unrestraint.
    2. be - li, "without" plus alah, "to
       ascend, meaning "without ascent"------
       Belial suggesting degradation.
    3. be - li, "without" plus ial, "to
       profit" or "to benefit"-----Belial
       suggesting worthless.

53. Philip E. Hughes, The Second Epistle to the Corinthians (Grand Rapids: Wm. B. Eerdmans, 1977), pp. 248-250, n. 12.

54. Vos op. cit., p. 100.

55. James B. Pritchard (ed.), Ancient Near Eastern Texts (Princeton: Princeton University Press, 1055), pp. 60-72; Alexander Heidel, The Babylonian Genesis (Chicago: The University of Chicago Press, 1950). In the Jewish apocalyptic literature, Belial stood for an adversary against God. The parallel of this sort of the Belial character can easily be found in the Near Eastern literature. Hence an attempt was made to trace the origin of the idea of Antichrist back to the ancient Babylonian myth of the contest between Marduk and Tiamat, the chaos-dragon which was recorded in Enuma-elish. The late Jewish apocalyptic idea of Belial was said to have been emerged under a strong influence of the Babylonian myth.

56. Boettner, op. cit., pp. 213-218.

57. E. J. Young, The Prophecy of Daniel (Grand Rapids: Wm. B. Eerdmans, 1953), p. 147.

58. For his political career see Wm. Tarn/ G.T. Griffith, Hellenistic Civilization (London: Edward Arnold LTD, 1959), pp. 33-35; 214 ff.

59. See for the classical exposition of the event, Edward Gibbon, The Decline and Fall of the Roman Empire (New York: Everyman's Library, 1963), 6 vols.

60. R. H. Charles, A Critical and Exegetical Commentary on the Revelation of St. John (Edinburgh: T. and T. Clark, 1956), Vol. 1, pp. 364-367; H.B. Swete, The Apocalypse of St. John (London: Macmillan Co., 1917), p. 176.

61. Cf. H. Berkhof, Christ the meaning of History (Richmond: John Knox, 1966), pp. 120, 280. Antichrist was also identified with the papacy. This was, in part, based on the numerical identity. The Latin title of the Pope, Vicarius Filii Dei Vicar of the Son of God has the numerical value of 666. But, in the light of the description of the man of lawlessness, this opinion must be oughtright rejected. Antichrist is notoriously anti-religious, while the Roman Pope is not.

62. Vos, op. cit., pp. 115-116; H.A.A. Kennedy, St. Paul's Conception of the Last Things, p. 218.

63. The subject of these verses has been much debated, and the choice is among Antiochus IV Epiphanes, the Romans, and Antichrist. See Young, op. cit., pp. 250-251.

64. A symbolic representation of victory by the power of a word goes back to creation. God created the world by His word. He spoke and it was done. This creation was mediated through the living word. Christ, Jn. 1:3; Heb. 1:2.

65. "The restraining hand" or "the restraint" has been variously interpreted as referring to: the Roman Empire, the Jewish state, the Holy Spirit, or the proclamation of the Gospel, cf. B.B. Warfield, Biblical and Theological Studies (Philadelphia: The Presbyterian and Reformed Publishing Co., 1952), pp. 472 ff.; Boettner, op. cit., pp. 213 ff.

66. For a comprehensive treatment of the signs of the times, see Hoekema, op. cit., pp. 129 ff.

CHAPTER V

The Historic-linear Eschatoogy (Cont)

The Millennium Question

Although "that day and that hour" of the
Advent were not revealed to Christians, those
"signs of the times," which we just reviewed,
were given to them for the sake of their
being always ready and watchful for the
Advent. When Christ returns, the present age
will come to its end, and the age to come
will begin its course. The Advent thus
stands at the midpoint between the present
age and the age to come. This was totally
unknown to the other eschatological systems
above in review.

The significance of Christ's Advent is
that the eschatological events, the resurrec-
tions of the just and unjust, the final
judgment, the cosmic transformation and
renewal, and the inauguration of the eternal
state, all are interlocked with the Advent.
Not all Christians, however, agree with this;
rather, different interpretations have been
presented. Broadly speaking, three general
systems were formulated: Premillennialism,
Amillennialism, and Post-millennialism. Our
term millennium was derived from two Latin
words: "mille," meaning thousand, and
"annum," meaning year. Thus the literal
meaning of millennium is a thousand years.
The Greek term for milennium is chilias, and
this word is used six times in the Bible, and
all are in the first seven verses of
Revelation 20. After this Greek word our
language chiliasm was created, and it has
been interchangeablely used with
millennialism.

Before we look into a number of related
issues with the millennium question, we first

131

make a brief outline of the three different
interpretations of millennium or the millennial kingdom of Christ.[1]

The Premillennialists in general
interpreted the word chilias in Rev.
20, as
meaning that the Advent will be followed by a
period of a 1000 years prior to the final
judgment and the inauguration of the eternal
state. The period of a 1000 years, or, in a
more common term, the millennial kingdom of
Christ is the period of the world-wide peace
and righteousness before the end of the present age. During the millennial kingdom
Christ rules as king in person on earth from
Jerusalem. Thus this was meant to suggest
that "the last day" of "the latter days" has
a length of the 1000 years.[2]

In this regard, the Premillennialists
interpretated literally a number of the
Scriptures. One of their favorite Scriptures
is the prophecy of Isaiah 11. In this
passage, the Prophet Isaiah prophesied that
the reign of the Messiah will be that of the
peace, tranquility, justice for all, the
natural ferocity of beasts would be quieted,
and he said: "They shall not hurt nor
destroy in all my mountain; for the earth
shall be full of the knowledge of the Lord,
as the waters cover the sea" (11:9). They
found, in many places in the Bible, the similar description of the Messianic kingdom.
For instance, the Psalmist said that the
dominion of the Messiah is from sea to sea
with all kings bowing down before Him, all
nations serving Him, and the earth filled
with the glory of the Lord. Then will be
fulfilled the desire of the nations for peace
and righteousness, for the knowledge of the
Lord, for economic justice, and for deliverance from satanic oppression and evil (Ps.
72).[3]

On the other hand, both the Amillenialists and Postmillennialists interpreted the word chilias figuratively, as meaning an indefinite long period but with beginning and end. For the Postmillennialists, however, as opposed to the Amillennialists, the millennium is a golden age of spiritual prosperity in the present age, and during the Millennium the world at large will enjoy a state of righteousness. This does not mean, however, that there ever will be a time on this earth when every person will be a Christian. Rather, it means that Christian principles will be the rule, and that Christ will return to a truly Christianized world. The present age gradually merges into this golden age, as an increasingly large proportion of the world's population is converted to Christianity.

A Postmillennialist once said that the millennium is "simply the full development of the kingdom of grace as it comes to fruition in this world. This kingdom begins very small, but it grows and eventually it dominates the whole earth."[4] He believed that during the millennium a state of rest and peace will exist throughout the church and over the whole world. In short, he looked for a golden age which will not be essentially different from our own so far as the basic facts of life are concerned. The millennium closes with, not follows, the Advent.

The Postmillennial interpretation of the millennium (chilias) was in part based on the symbolism in the book of Revelation. The number ten stands for rounded totals (e.g. the Ten Commandments; the ten plagues). The cube, with all side equal, symbolizes perfection. The Holy of Holies was ten cubits long, ten cubits wide, and ten cubits high. The number 1000 is the cube of ten and symbolizes vastness of number or time. A 1000 years symbolically suggests a definitely

133

limited period, during which certain events happen and after which certain other events are to follow.[5]

From the same Scriptures, upon which the Premillennialists had worked for their position, the Postmillennialists found the descriptions of the millennial golden age.[6] Those Scriptures seem to point out the fact that the reign of Christ is now being extended in the world through the preaching of the Gospel and the saving work of the Holy Spirit in the hearts of individuals, and that the world eventually will be christianized and will see the final triumph of the Gospel in the present age just prior to the Advent.

One of their favorite Scriptures is found in Isaiah 2: 2, 3:

> And it shall come to pass in the last days, that the mountain of the Lord's house shall be established in the top of the mountains, and shall be exalted above the hills; and all nations shall flow unto it. And many people shall go and say, Come ye, and let us go up the house of the God of Jacob; and he will teach us of his ways, and we will walk in his paths: for out of Zion shall go forth the law, and the word of the Lord from Jerusalem.

In Heb. 12:22, "mountain Zion" is spiritualized to mean the church. Hence the Postmillennialists had taken the prophecy as meaning that "the Church, having attained a position so that it stands out like a mountian on a plain, will be prominent and regulative in all world affairs."[7] Dan. 2:44 seems to teach the same truth. In this passage, "the stone cut out without hands" represents a spiritual kingdom, which God Himself will set up and which figuratively

134

will become a great mountain and will fill the entire earth. The Christian church is an institution not of human but of divine origin and therefore is described in Daniel's passage as "the stone cut out wihtout hands," and thus the Christian church represents a spiritual kingdom. In short, Daniel saw that the church was destined to break all the anti-Christian kingdoms and transform them.[8]

In many places the Bible speaks of the universal triumphant reign of Christ (e.g. Num. 14:21; Ps. 2:8; 22:22-29; 72; Isa. 2:2-4; 11:6-9; 65-66; Jer. 31:31-34; Zech. 9:9-10; 13:1; 14:9; Matt. 13:33; Rev. 7:9, 10:19: 11-21). From these passages one could argue for the golden age, "since they cannot refer to a post-adventual reign of Christ and because nothing that has taken place in history does justice to the glory of the prophetic vision, the golden age must be yet future, but prior to Messiah's return."[9] The Postmillennialists saw, in the Great Commission to proclaim the Gospel to all nations (Matt. 28:18-19), a promise that the effectual evangelization of all the nations will be completed before Christ's return.[10]

The Amillennialists disagreed with the Postmillennialists as to the golden age. The present world is not to merge into the golden age before the Advent. Rather, the present world continues much as it now is, with a parallel and continuous development of both good and evil. Some of the Amillennialists understood chilias as referring to the entire Christian era from His ascension to Advent; others applied it to a relatively Christian and peaceful era,[11] and still others to the intermediate state, in which the souls of the departed saints reign with Christ. They generally interpreted many of those Scriptures, to which both the Pre-and Postmillennialists made appeal, as describing figuratively the consummation and the eternal state.

Both A- and Postmillennialisms are in agreement, as opposed to Premillennialism, that the Advent will bring the present age to its end and will usher in the final judgment and the eternal state, as Christ said: "And, behold, I come quickly; and my reward is with me, to give every man according to his work shall be. I am Alpha and Omega, the Beginning and the end, the first and the last" (Rev. 22: 12, 13).

On the other hand, both Pre- and Amillennialisms are in agreement, as opposed to Postmillennialism, that the prior to the Advent there will be a widespread apostasy which will be climaxed by the appearance of the personal Antichrist, and a great tribulation.

On the issue of the great tribulation, Premillennialism itself became divided into historic-Premillennialism and Dispensationalism. The former held that believers living at the Advent will go through the great tribulation. At the Advent, all believers, the dead first being bodily resurrected and the living being transformed, will unite with the coming Lord and enter the millennial kingdom. On the other hand, the Dispensationalists advocated the two stages of the Advent: rapture and revelation. The rapture is the coming of Christ for His people, at which time all believers will be caught up in their resurrected or transformed bodies to meet Christ in the air. This rapture will take place prior to the great tribulation, and the raptured saints will remain in the air for a period of seven years (Dan. 9:27). During this short period Antichrist rules on the earth, and the woes spoken of in the book of Revelation (6-19) fall on the inhabitants of the earth. Thus the raptured saints or church will not suffer the great tribulation. At the end of seven years, Christ and His raptured saints return to the earth. This return is called revelation. At the revelation Christ overpowers Antichrist, defeats the enemies of His people in the battle of Armageddon (Rev. 16:16), and establishes His millennial kingdom on the earth. The Jews are to be converted at the revelation to have a prominent place in the millennial kingdom.

With this brief outline, we now turn to some of the key issues, to which these three differenet millennailisms addressed themselves.

1. The binding of Satan a thousand years

Our text says:

> And he (an angel) laid hold on the dragon, that old serpent, which is the Devil, and Satan, and bound him a thousand years, And cast him into the bottomless pit, and shut him up, and set a seal upon him, that he should deceive the nations no more, till the thousand years should be fulfilled: and after that he must be loosed a little season (Rev. 20:2. 3).

In this passage, the purpose of the binding and incarceration of Satan in the "bottomless pit" a thousand years was that he should deceive the nations no more for a thousand year period. This idea of the deception of the nations reappears after Satan is loosed at the end of the millennium (20:8). According to Premillennialism, this suggests that this binding is different from the binding of Satan accomplished by Jesus in His earthly ministry. They argued that the victory Jesus won over Satan was won once and for all (Matt. 12:28, 29), and that Satan will never be loosed from bondage to Christ which was won by His death and resurrection.[12] They also saw in this part of the book of Revelation an order of the chronological sequence. Chapter 19 contains a vivid picture of Christ's complete victory over the enemies of His people; chapter 20 states events which follow the Advent.

Notwithstanding, they would recognize the fact that the Apostle John in writing the book of Revelation does not always follow the order of time. If the chronological order of events to be consistently maintained, the result will be fatal, because the solemnization of the bride's marriage with the Lamb (19:5 ff.) is placed subsequent to the millennium and even subsequent to the general resurrection. After the period of conflict is entirely closed and the final rewards have been dispensed, we read that the holy city, the new Jerusalem, appears descending out of heaven as a bride adorned for her husband (21:2). In 19:7, the time for the marriage has come.

In disagreement with the Premillennialists, both the A- and Postmillennialists hold that the binding of Satan in our text and that accomplished by Jesus' own death and resurrection are the same. This difference basically resulted from a different understanding of the meaning of "binding." Although some of the Premillennialists concede that the binding of Satan is "a symbolic way of describing a curbing of his power and authority, and that it does not mean his complete immobility,"[13] the Premillennialists by and large conceive of the binding of Satan as the binding to the degree of being completely inactive.[14]

Both the A- and Postmillennialists reasoned for the restricting of Satan's power from the general use of the word "to bind." The binding in our general use always means the limitation of power in some way. For

138

instance, when men took an oath, they agreed
to limit their power and rights, but they
live their lives as human beings.[15]
Likewise the binding of Satan meant
restricting Satan not in every way but only
in regard to his work of deceiving the
nations. According to some of the A- and
Postmillennialists, the implication here is
that Satan no longer is able to prevent the
Gospel being proclaimed to the nations. This
was based on the Old Testament use of
"nation." In the Old Testament, the word
"nation" is used for the Gentile people as
distinguished from the Israelites. During
the Old Testament dispensation the Gentiles
were deceived by Satan, and salvation was
particularistic and limited to God's chosen
covenant people. With Christ's death and
resurrection, a new era set in, and Satan is
bound by Jesus during His earthly
ministry.[16] From the beginning of the new
era the Gospel is to be proclaimed to all
nations, and Satan is powerless to prevent
it.

This was taught in a number of the
Scriptures. Matt. 12:28, 29, in connection
with the coming of the kingdom of God, refer
to a binding of Satan, and as a strong man is
bound and then is truly powerless, so Satan
is bound and powerless. Col. 2:15 refers to
Satan being disarmed. John 12:31 and Rev.
12:9 speak of the Devil being cast out during
Christ's earthly ministry. Satan, being
unable to do to the people of God what he
craves to inflict upon them, confers his
power to "the beast," that is, Antichrist,
which arises out of the "sea" (Rev. 12:17;
13:1-2). Here Satan was handicapped, but we
are left to guess why. Only in 20:1-3 do
we learn about his being bound, and know that
this must have happened "a thousand years"
before the end of Antichrist, not after
Antichrist and his false prophet were cast
into "the lake of fire" (19:20).[17]

Thus the binding of Satan was linked closely with Christ's atonement on the cross. Our text speaks of the "loosing" of Satan when a 1000 years is over. This might suggest the annulment of His atonement, or at least a time when it becomes ineffective in restricting Satan's power.[18] This difficulty, however, is apparent. The loosing of Satan for a short season is closely related to his final undoing, for which the Advent also will take place (Rev. 20: 7-15).

It has been suggested that the two passages, Rev. 20:2-3 and 20:8, should be read together in order to find the real meaning of the binding of Satan. Rev. 20:8 says: "And (Satan) shall go out to deceive the nations which are in the four quarters of the earth, Gog and Magog, to gather them together to battle." This is done after Satan once again is loosed at the end of a 1000 years, and it claims that this verse provides the meaning of the binding of Satan, namely, Satan cannot gather the nations for the final cataclysm until a 1000 year period is fulfilled.[19]

According to a leading Postmillennialist, Benjamin B. Warfield, in the binding of Satan, the time-element and chronolgoical succession belong to the symbol, not to the thing symbolized. In reality, the binding and loosing of Satan are with reference to a sphere, not for a season. The loosing of Satan thus is not after a period but in another sphere; it is not subsequence but exteriority that is implied. What actually happens in the binding of Satan happens not to Satan but to the saints, namely, the saints described are removed from the sphere of Satan's assaults. The saints are free from all access of Satan because he is bound with respect to them.[20]

2. The reigning with Christ

Our text says:

> And they lived and reigned with
> Christ a thousand years. But the
> rest of the dead lived not again
> until the thousand years were
> finished. This is the first
> resurrection. Blessed and holy is
> he that hath part in the first
> resurrection: on such the second
> death hath no power, but they shall
> be priests of God and of Christ, and
> shall reign with him a thousand
> years (Rev. 20:4 b-6).

In these verses, we notice the different
tenses. In verse 6, "they shall reign" is
the aoristic future and in verse 4 b, "they
reigned" is the historical aorist (past).
However both the aoristic future and the
hitorical aorist express an action viewed in
its entirety as an event or thing
accomplished.[21]

The Apostle John here stated that the
reigning with Christ is the historically
accomplished thing. The actuality and eventuation of this accomplished thing, according
to premillennialism, will take place with
the Advent when Satan will be bound a
thousand years. Thus the reigning with
Christ a 1000 years simply meant the millennial kingdom which Christ will establish at
His Advent.

But the A- and Postmillennialists
interpreted our text differently. Our text
says that those who shall reign with Christ a
thousand yeas are also the ones who shall be
priests of God and of Christ. These two
issues--the reigning with Christ and the
priesthood--are inseparably related to

141

constitute one issue. This is borne out in the fact that believers are made kings and priests unto God by Jesus Christ through His atoning work. Rev. 1:6 and 5:9, 10 testify to this: "For thou was slain and hast redeemed us to God by thy blood out of every kindred, and tongue, and people, and nation; and hast made us unto our God kings and priests, and they shall reign on the earth" (5:9, 10). Thus the kingship and priesthood, that is the kingdom of priests is the accomplished fact through the blood of Christ. The only question before us is when the actualization of this special privilege will occur for believers. In other words, the question has to do with "realized" or "unrealized." According to A-and Postmillennialisms, as opposed to Premillennialism, it is present and realized, not in the future. The kingdom of priests is a present reality.

When the Apostle John spoke of our text (Rev. 20: 4b-6), he undoubtedly had in mind the status of Israel which was defined in these words: "And ye shall be unto me a kingdom of priests and an holy nation" (Exod. 19:6). In this verse, the kingdom signifies both kingship as the embodiment of a royal supremacy, exaltation, and dignity, and the union between a king and subject. Israel was chosen to be a royal body to render the priestly service unto God. When Israel was chosen to be the kingdom of priests, God entrusted upon her a mission of priesthood. Thus the kingdom of priests suggests that her mission was universalistic in its nature and scope: Israel was to render the priestly service unto God on behalf of all mankind. In the execution of this mission, Israel as "an holy nation" was to follow a particular way of life, a life of holiness, which was to mark her off as a distinct people among nations. This was to make known to nations that only Yahweh is holy God and the Lord.[22] Thus the election of Israel to be the kingdom of

142

priests was in response to the divine promise made to Abraham: "In thee shall all families of the earth be blessed" (Gen. 12:3).

In the light of this Old Testament teaching of the Abrahamic covenant, it becomes very clear that "the priests of God and of Christ" and the reigning with Christ constitute one present reality, the kingdom of priests of believers. The Apostle Peter confirms this in his words: "Ye also, as lively stone, are built up a spiritual house, an holy priesthood, to offer up spiritual sacrifices, acceptable to God by Jesus Christ" (I Pet. 2:5), and "But ye are a chosen generation, a royal priesthood, an holy nation, a peculiar people; that ye should shew forth the praises of him who hath called you out of darkness into his marvelous light" (v. 9).[23]

Some scholars regarded the reigning with Christ as the restoration in heaven of man's dominion over nature which was lost in paradise. However, its full consummation is attained after the resurrection at the advent.[24]

Since in our text the Apostle John does not mention the Advent at all, and he does not say that the reigning with Christ takes place on the earth, one concluded that it may well be located in heaven.[25]

In any case, the reigning with Christ has two aspects: on the part of believers, it means the kingdom of priests, i.e. the royal-priestly service; on the part of Christ, it means the Messianic reign. In this Messianic kingdom believers, as its citizens and priests, serve Him in worship, witness, and mercy to all nations.

Jesus promised "to him that overcometh will I grant to sit with me in my throne,

even as I also overcome, and am set down with
my Father in his throne" (Rev. 3:21). This
metaphorical language describes the ultimate
victory of Christ's reign. Here the victory
of Christ is pictured as an enthronement with
His Father upon His Father's throne. This
enthronement is usually stated as the sitting
"at the right hand" of God the Father (e.g.
Acts 2:34; Rom. 8:34; Eph. 1:20; Col. 3:1;
Heb. 1:3; 8:1; 10:12; 12:2; 1 Pet. 3:22).
Christ is already enthroned, and the
Messianic rule has already begun. Therefore,
after Christ's resurrection and ascension,
St. Peter announced to his followers that
"God hath made that same Jesus, whom ye have
crucified, both Lord and Christ" (Acts 2:36).

The reigning with Christ, on the part of
Christ, meant in specific manner the subjugation of "authorities and powers and
rules" (Cor. 15:24; 1 Pet. 3:22), and of the
last enemy, "the death" (1 Cor. 15:26b; Rev.
20:14; Ps. 110:1-2).[26] The reigning with
Christ, on the part of believers and in the
objective realm, especially meant the reward
of "the everlasting inheritance." This reward
could not be thought of apart from Christ's
own inheritance, because He is "heir of all
things" (Heb. 1:2). Jesus Christ, through
His "passive" and "active" obedience to His
Father, obtained for believers "heir of all
things." "Christ as the vicar of his people
came under the curse and condemnation due to
sin ("pasive" obedience) and he also
fulfilled the law of God in all its positive
requirements" ("active" obedience).[27] In
other words, the reigning with Christ, on the
part of His people, meant "joint-heirs with
Christ." Therefore St. Paul said: "The
Spirit itself beareth witness with our
spirit, that we are the children of God: And
if children, then heirs; heirs of God, and
joint-heirs with Christ; if so be that we
suffer with him, that we may be also
glorified together" (Rom. 8: 16, 17).[28]

We have just noted that the reigning with
Christ has the two aspects: the present,
realized and subjective element of the royal
priesthood, and the future, unrealized and
objective element of inheritance. The
prophet Isaiah must have this in mind when he
said: "But ye shall be named the priests of
the Lord: men shall call you the ministers
of our God: ye shall eat the riches of the
Gentiles, and in their glory shall ye boast
yourselves" (61:6). Also, the Apostle John
summed up these two aspects in these words:
"He that overcometh shall inherit all things,
and I will be his God, and he shall be my
son" (Rev. 21:7), and "there shall be no
night there (in the city of God), ... for the
Lord God giveth them light, and they shall
reign for ever and ever" (Rev. 22:5). The
future phase of the reigning with Christ has
the characteristics of "shepherding"
(poimanei) with "a rod of iron" and "ruling
over the twelve tribes" (Matt. 19:28). This
we shall discuss later when we come to the
issue of the final judgment.

3. The first resurrection

Our text says:

> And they lived and reigned with
> Christ a thousand years. But the
> rest of the dead lived not again
> until the thousand yeas were
> finished. This is the first
> resurrection (Rev. 20: 4b-5).

Our text clearly states that the reigning
with Christ a thousand years is the first
resurrection. That is to say, the reigning
with Christ a thousand years and the first
resurrection are inseparable. In this proper
perspective, our choice of the meaning of
"the first resurrection" is among these

three: (1) the bodily resurrection of all deceased believers at the Advent, (2) the spiritual resurrection of all believers, and (3) the spiritual and bodily resurrection of all believers. The Premillennialists pointed out, as they favored the first meaning, that "the crux of the entire exegetical problem (of the first resurrection) is the meaning of the sentence: "they lived and reigned with Christ a thousand years."[29] The same verb "to live" (zao) again appears in verse five: "the rest of the dead lived not again." The latter sentence seems to imply the bodily resurrection. It has been reasoned that in the same context the same word must be taken with the same meaning.[30] As the sentence, "the rest of dead lived not again," implies the bodily resurrection, so the sentence, "they lived and reigned with Christ a thousand years," implies the bodily resurrection. This bodily resurrection in our passage is called the first resurrection. In short, according to Premillennialism, our passage teaches us that at the beginning of the millennial period, part of the dead will come to life, i.e. the bodily resurrection; at its conclusion, the rest of the dead will come to life again.[31]

We ought to remark that in the New Testament there is no Greek verb which exclusively means "to raise from the dead," but several verbs are used.[32] In the New Testament, the verb zao ("to live") is used more often, however. Each determines its meaning in the context, and the context provides a clue for two different meanings of the same word, if there is any variation. For instance, in Jn. 5: 25-29, the context makes it clear that the references are to those who are spiritually dead and to the physically dead. In Rev. 20: 4-6, there is no such contextual clue for the different references in the use of the verb "to live." This contextual situation seems to favor the Premillennial interpretation of "the first resurrection."

The Premillennial interpretation of
"the first resurrection," however, is not
without some difficulties. Our text does not
say that "But the rest of the dead lived not
again until the thousand years were
finished," but it says that "But the rest of
the dead lived not until, or up to, the point
of the completion of the thousand years."
This is equivalent to saying that "the second
death (v.6) had power on the rest of the dead
during the thousand year period." That is to
say, those on whom the second death has power
are never redeemed from its power. So "the
rest of the dead did not live until the
thousand years were finished, nor did they
live after the thousand years were finished."
Also, the word "until" does not of itself
imply that a change occurs after the point to
which it refers is reached (cf. Rom 5:13).[33]

Furthermore, the first resurrection and
the second death are in contrast. The second
death figuratively and metaphorically refers
to the eternal condemnation (Rev. 20:14).
Therefore it is very natural to understand
the first resurrection also figuratively and
metaphorically. The second death was so
named in order to distinguish it from our
natural physical death, and the first
resurrection was so called in order to
distinguish it from the resurrection of our
body which occurs later.[34]

Another difficulty was created when the
Premillennialists separated between the
resurrection of believers and that of unbelievers by the 1000 year period. But, this
went counter the Apostle John, who said:
"Marvel not at this: for the hour is coming,
in the which all that are in the graves shall
hear his voice, and shall come forth; they
that have done good, unto the resurrection of
life; and they that have done evil, unto the
resurrection of damnation." Here both the
resurrection of life and the resurrection of

damnation are to take place at the same time
when "the hour is coming." Both resurrec-
tions are coeval with the coming of "the
hour," on that hour all who are in the graves
shall hear the voice of Jesus Christ (Dan.
12: 1-2).

The choice of the second meaning, the
spiritual resurrection of all believers,
was made on the use of the word "throne." In
the book of Revelation, the word "throne" is
employed 47 times, and all but three of them
(2:13; 13:2; 16:10) appear to be in heaven.
In Rev. 20: 1-3, the locality of St. John's
vision was on the earth; in verses 4-6, the
locality was shifted to heaven. The verses
1-3 describe what happens on earth during the
1000 year period, and the verses 4-6 depict
what happens in heaven during the same 1000
year period. In St. John's description,
"setting on throne" is a concrete way of
expressing the thought that they are reigning
with Christ.[35] In that vision St. John saw
believers who are crowned by their being
taken to heaven to be with Christ, not in the
bodily resurrection, but in the sense that
they are enjoying life in heaven in
fellowhsip with Christ. That is to say, he
saw them living and reigning with Christ
during the intermediate state.[36]

A question has been raised whether or
not, in the New Testament, the verb zao ("to
live") is used to describe souls living on
after the physical death.[37] We find a positive answer to this question in these words:
"For he is not a God of the dead, but of the
living: for all live unto him" (Lk. 20:38).
This was Christ's answer to the Sadducees who
denied not only the resurrection of the body
but also the continued existence of the soul
after death.[38] In order to correct this
denial, Jesus said these words. His words
imply that in some sense the patriarchs,
Abraham, Isaac, and Jacob, are living even

148

now, after their death, but before their
resurrection. This is also suggested in
these words: "And whoever liveth and
believeth in me shall never die" (Jn.
11:25-26).

The third alternative of the spiritual
and bodily resurrection for the meaning of
the first resurrection was simply based on
the previous exposition of the meaning of the
reigning with Christ. The reigning with
Chirst is the continual process toward the
consummation, and has three phases: the
first phase on the earth, the second phase in
heaven, and the third phase on the new heaven
and new earth. Although the immediate
reference of the first resurrection in our
Revelation passage is to the second phase, it
would not be necessary to restrict its
reference to the living and reigning with
Christ in heaven.

In many places in the New Testament, the
first phase of the first resurrection was
described as being buried and raised with
Christ in baptism.[39] For example:

> We are burieth with him by baptism
> into death: that like as Christ was
> raised up from the dead ... (Rom.
> 6:4) And hath raised us up
> together, and made us sit together
> in heavenly places in Christ Jesus
> (Eph. 2:6). Buried with him in
> baptism, wherein also ye are risen
> with him through faith of the opera-
> tion of God, who hath raised him
> from the dead. And you, being dead
> in your sins and the uncircumcision
> of your flesh, hath he quickened
> together with him, having forgiven
> you all tresspasses (Col. 2: 12,
> 13).[40]

149

Thus the reigning with Christ, that is, the first phase of the first resurrection simply meant the present life of believers on earth. In reference to the first and second phases of the reigning with Christ, "the first resurrection" meant the spiritual resurrection on earth and in heaven. The third phase refers to the bodily resurrection of all the deceased saints and the bodily transformation of all living believers at the Advent.

According to Premillennialism, beside our Revelation passage 20:1-6, one more Scripture in the New Testament teaches the earthly millennial kingdom coming after the Advent, namely, 1 Cor. 15:20-28.[41] In this passage, St. Paul concerned himself with the Christians who did believe in the bodily resurrection of Christ, but no longer expected a bodily resurrection of believers. Against this error, St. Paul set forth the divine order of things: Christ, the firstfruits, was raised first; after that, at the parousia, believers be raised, and "then cometh the end, when he shall have delivered up the kingdom to God, even the Father" (v. 24).

In this passage, the word "then" (eita) was interpreted to mean "later" in the sense of a chronological interval. Thus the passage would read: "Christ having been the first to rise, and afterwards Christ's people rising at His return, later on comes the rest of the remainder of the dead." The "end" was also translated "the rest" or "the remainder."[42] In the New Testament, the word "then" occurs ten times; some of them indicate the time-lapse. For instance, in the parable of the sower (Lk. 8: 4-15), the seed fallen on the hard soil was trodden under feet, and "then" (v. 12) the birds devoured it. Jesus "was seen of Cephus, then of the twelves: ...after that he was seen of James, then of

all the apostles" (1 Cor. 15: 5, 7). "For
Adam was first formed, then Eve" (1 Tim.
2:13). However, we have to admit that the
word "then" (eita) may mean sequence with or
without chronological interval. The latter
case is also well demonstrated. For
instance, while Jesus was on the cross, after
He said to His mother, "Behold thy son!
then he said to John behold thy mother!"
Even in the parable of the sower, the meaning
of "then," rather, is "the next."

We have made thus a long parenthesis to
discuss some of the key issues related to the
millennium question. All the three systems
of millennialism had merits and shortcomings;
nevertheless, each legitimately could claim
to be the biblical teaching. On this premise
the present exegesis commended neo-Amillen-
nialism coming in between Amillennialism
and Postmillennialism, especially in respect
with the meaning of "the first resurrection,"
as it has the three phases of the living and
reigning with Christ, that is, the first
resurrection on earth, in heaven (the intermediate state), and in the new heaven and the
new earth.

The Advent will close the present age and
usher in the age to come. Jesus therefore
said: "Behold, I come quickly; and my reward
is with me, to give every man according as
his work shall be. I am Alpha and Omega, the
beginning and the end, the first and the
last" (Rev. 22: 12-13; 1:17; 2:8; 1:8; 21:6).
When He comes again, "the last trump" will be
blown, and at that moment the resurrection of
the righteous occurs (1 Cor. 15:52). This is
"the last trump," and there can be no other
trump. "The last trump" signals "the end" of
the present age.[43]

Before the arrival of "the end," toward
which now the present age moves on, Christ
must have put down all "rule, authority, and

151

power" (1 Cor. 15:24). Christ's reign of conques must last until He shall have put all enemies under His feet, and "the last enemy" to be destroyed is death (1 Cor. 15:26). His reign of conquest moves on, however, in the superterrestrial sphere of the world of spirits and so unobservable by natural man. It is a progressive subjugation of enemies leading up to "the end," to the consummation, at which point "the former things are passed away" (Rev. 21:4). Both St. Paul and St. John underlay the fact that "the end" cannot be separated from the Advent. Rather, "the end" is brought into collocation with the Advent and the day of the Lord for which believers earnestly await (1 Cor. 1:6-8).

The Advent is the hope of Christians for the reigning with Christ, the third and the last phase of the first resurrection. Before the coming of this "end," presently believers experience and enjoy the reigning with Christ; this is the first phase of the first resurrection. When anyone believes in Christ, he is buried in baptism and raised to reign with Christ, who is in heaven. When believers died their soul or spirit enters the second phase of the first resurrection in heaven. This was what the Apostle John saw in his vision (Rev. 20: 4-6). Thus the Judeo-Christian perspective of our physical death is quite different from the other eschatologies. The souls of believers are not doomed into the depth of the earth which the others variously called "the land of no return," nirvana, nothingness, or void.

The Apostle John saw those who sat upon the throne in heaven and the souls of those who were martyred as witness of Jesus (Rev. 20:4). The martyrs are conscious and capable of being addressed (Rev. 6: 9-11). They were wearing the white robes and "resting." This suggests that they are enjoying a provisional

kind of blessedness during the second phase
of the first resurrection, that is, in the
intermediate state. They look forward to the
final bodily resurrection, that is, the third
phase of the first resurrection in the eternal state, and so they said with a loud voice:
"How long, O Lord, holy and true, dost thou
not judge and avenge our blood on them that
dwell on the earth?" (Rev. 6:10).

Jesus spoke of death as "fall asleep"
(Jn. 11:11-13) in order to direct our atten-
tion to His victory over death and to the
power of the Holy Spirit which, in figuratively speaking, wakes up him from sleep.[44]
When Christians die, they do not enter the
state of soul-sleep in their graves until the
Advent. The soul-sleep idea is more or less
pagan thought. This is seen in the promise
which Jesus on the cross made to a thief that
he will be with Him in paradise (Lk. 23:42-43).
Here "paradise" meant heaven, the realm of
the blessed dead and the special habitation
of God (2 Cor. 12:4; Rev. 2:7). This promise
denied the idea of soul-sleep, because if the
thief after death would totally be unaware of
being with Christ in paradise, for what would
be the point of saying this promise? For the
Apostle Paul "to live is Christ, and to die
is gain" (Phil. 1:22, 23-24). He also should
deny the idea of soul-sleep, because how
could soul-sleep be "gain" and "far better"
than the present state, in which he had
conscious, though imperfect, fellowship with
Christ?

While the Apostle Paul contended with the
present reality that "to abide in the flesh is
more needful" (Phil. 1:24) for the Philippian
Christians, he still had an earnest desire to
be away from the body and at home with the
Lord (2 Cor. 5:1-8), because our present
fellowship with the Lord still leaves much to
be desired. In death, the struggle against
sin and tribulation comes to an end; in death

153

there is "a vision of peace," but also a vision of God, when faith becomes sight. Preently believers "walk by faith," but in the intermediate state after death they "walk by sight." On earth the believers hope but do not see, whereas in death, they witness what they have long expected.

This idea of the intermediate state is one of the many features of the historic-linear eschatology which makes it distinctive from the others. This is surely not a Platonic idea as one might think it to be. The Platonic concept of immortality of soul must be taken from the point of view of the circular time-concept. The soul in its view simply disappears into a void, and looses self-consciousness. For the pagans at their best, they rely on karma ("action"), the principle of cause-effect, which is said to determine a form of being in a series of rebirths or seemingly endless transmigration.

In short, the historic-linear eschatology teaches us that death does not terminate human existence. After death a person does not go totally out of existence but goes to Sheol, "a grave or a realm of the dead."[45] In this realm, the ungodly shall remain and suffer torment, even before the resurrection of the body (Lk. 16:19-31). God's people, however, knowing that Christ was not abandoned to the realm of the dead, have the firm hope that they too shall be delivered from the power of the death and that they will continue to reign with Christ in heaven (paradise). This intermediate state in heaven is provisional, temporary and incomplete, because man is not totally man apart from the body. Man is body-and-soul or spirit, or man is body-and-soul-and-spirit.[46] The Judeo-Christian hope is not a hope for a mere continual existence of the soul alone but for the resurrection of the body.[47]

This Judeo-Christian hope is totally
distinctive as compared to others beliefs,
such as that of Greeks, who believed that
man's body is evil and is a hindrance to his
full existence. Hence at death the body
disintegrates while the soul vanishes into an
untouchable realm.

The Resurrection of the Body and

the Final Judgment

The resurrection and judgment are the two
correlated eschatological acts at the Advent.
The resurrection sets in motion and judgment
seals what one has received in the
ressurection. These two processes determine
and establish the status of man in a new
order of affairs in eternity.

In the resurrection, Christians will
receive the "spiritual" (pneumatikon) body.
But the resurrection body does not mean to be
constituted of pneuma, but adapted to all
that the life of God's pneuma means.[48] In
order to characterize its qualities, St.
Paul placed the resurrection body in contrast
with the "physical" (psychikon) body (1 Cor.
15:42-43). The resurrection body in nature
is imperishable, glorious and powerful, and
in origin, of heaven like Christ's body (1
Cor. 15:45-49), yet still a body, while the
"physical" (Psychikon) body in nature is
perishable, dishonoring and weak, and in
origin, of dust like Adams' body. While the
physical body adapted to life in the present
age, the spiritual body (pneumatikon soma)
adapted to life in the age to come. This
shows the imperative and absolute necessity
of the resurrection body. It is not possible
for us in our present state, that is, in the
natural or physical body, to inherit the full

blessings of life in the age to come. There must be a change from the physical body to the spiritual body (1 Cor. 15:50).

Believers living at the time of the Advent will be transformed and glorified to be adapted to life in the age to come (1 Cor. 15:51; 2 Cor. 3:18; Phil. 3:21). Both the resurrection and transformation result in the same "spiritual body" bearing after Christ's own image which Christ Himself obtained in His own resurrection (1 Cor. 15:49). There is an intimated relation between Christ's resurrection and the believer's resurrection. The same power that raised Christ will raise up His people (1 Cor. 6:14; 2 Cor. 4:14). Christ's resurrection is itself the first act of the final resurrection, the pledge and guarantee of the future resurrection of believers – Christ is the "first fruits" and the "first born" (1 Cor. 15:20; 1 Th. 4:16; Col. 1:18; cf. Rom. 8:29; Jn. 14:19).

The Bible does not say much about what the resurrection body looks like. It simply says that the resurrection body is similar to angels (Matt. 22:30; Mark 12:25; Lk. 20:35). The similarity to angels, however, applies only to the point being made, not to the absence of physical bodies. The teaching here does not imply that there will be no sex difference in the life to come, but implies that the institution of marriage will no longer be in existence, since there will be no need to bring new children.[49] St. Paul stressed the continuity between the present physical body and the future resurrection body (1 Cor. 15:20 ff.) This emphasis could easily be understood by the fact that the resurrection body is like that of Christ which was physical (Jn. 20:17, 27; Lk. 24: 38-43), and by the fact that the word "spiritual" (Pneumatikon) does not describe that which is nonmaterial or nonphysical (1 Cor. 2:14-15). The word "spiritual" does not

mean nonphysical; rather it means someone who
is guided by the Holy Spirit, at least in
principle, in distinction from someone who is
guided only by his material impulse.[50] The
very thought of immaterialness or absence of
physical destiny in the state of the
resurrection, therefore, ought to be care-
fully removed from the Judeo-Christian
eschatology. The absence of physical destiny
in the future state of being is a completely
pagan idea.

For Christians the resurrection is a
reward for the incurring of danger and the
daily dying undergone, and for the labor
accomplished (1 Cor. 15:58). Also, the
resurrection for them is the final removal of
the condemnation of sin. Therefore it is
pictured as the swallowing up of death in
victory (1 Cor. 15:55-57). On the other
hand, the resurrection of the unjust simply
is a prelude to the final judgment and
condemnation.

Christ is also coming for the final
judgment. He will come to judge both the
good and evil on "the day of wrath," when
God's righteous judgment will be revealed.[51]
God the Father is the judge, but He judges
through the Son, as He is the creator, but He
creates through the Son.[52] Christ will be
assisted in the work of judging by angels and
saints (Matt. 13:41-43; 19;28; 24:31; 25:31;
1 Cor. 6:2-3; Rev. 2:26, 27). He will judge
all according to their works, including even
angels (1 Cor. 6:2-3; 2 Pet. 2:4; Jude 6).[53]
He will judge all things which have been done
during this present life (2 Cor. 5:10). All
things inlcude a person's words, thoughts
and deeds.[54]

However, the distinction between the
judgment according to their work and salvation on account of good works must be fully
appreciated. The notion that salvation on

account of good works is non-Judeo-Christian.
The good works spoken of in the final judgement are not to be construed as the meriting
of good for receiving the blessings of eternal
life but rather as the evidence of a genuine
faith in Christ.
The real reason for the final judgment
according to their works, even though salvation comes through faith in Christ and is
never earned by work, ought to be found in
the fact that faith and good works are inseparably associated. As St. James taught us,
faith must reveal itself in works, and works,
in turn, are the evidence of true faith
(James 2:18, 26; Gal. 5:6; Matt. 7:21). The
judgment according to their works presupposes
the pretentious faith, which is not a genuine
and living faith. In a true sense, the
judgment according to their works is a
judgment about faith as revealed in its
evidence.[55]

Christ will judge all according to the
revealed will of God the Father, but this
standard will not be the same for all. The
judgment of those outside the pole of the
Gospel must be according to their works (Rom.
1:20; 2:13, 14, 15). The judgment of those
inside the pole of the Gospel who rejected
the Gospel will be according to the law
naturally and specially revealed and the
Gospel they rejected. Those who have
received the full revelation of God's will in
both the Old and New Testaments will be
judged by their responses to the entire
Scripture (Lk. 16:19 ff.). There will therefore be "graduation" in the suffering of the
lost (Lk. 12:47-48).

The ultimate purpose of the final
judgment is the vindication of God's own
glory; everyhting must be perfectly adjudi-
cated to the vindication of God's glory (Rom.
3:4). The final judgment is to display the
sovereignty and glory of God in the revela-

tion of the final destiny of each person,
whose final destiny, up to this point, has
been hidden. In this revelation of the final
destiny of each individual, His grace will be
manifested in the consummation of the salvation of His people, and His justice will be
manifested in the condemnation of the enemies
of His people. Thus the central issue on the
day of the final judgment is not the destinies of individuals but the glory of God.[56]

A New Heaven and A New Earth

(the third phase of the reigning with Christ)

The final judgment seals what the
resurrection sets in, namely, the resurrection of the just unto eternal life, the
resurrection of the unjust unto eternal
condemnation, and the inauguration of a new
heaven and a new earth. The goal of redemption is nothing less than the cosmic redemption or the cosmic renewal. Since man's fall
into sin affected not only life but also the
rest of creation (Gen. 3:17-18), redemption
from sin involves the totality of God's
creation (Rom. 8:19-23). The cosmic redemption is coupled with the fact that Christ is the
author of creation as well as redemption
(Col. 1:16-20; Eph. 1:9-10). Nothing short
of the total deliverance of creation from its
"bondage to decay" will satisfy the redemptive purpose of God.

Jesus also spoke of the "regeneration"
(palingenesia) of the world (Matt. 19:28).
Josephus used the same word palingenesia
interchangeably with apokatastasis,
"restoration."[57] The cosmic renewal will be
a cataclysmic event as Christ prophesied:
"Immediately after the tribulation of these
days shall the sun be darkened, and the moon
shall not give her light, and the stars shall

fall from heaven, and the powers of the heavens shall be shaken" (Matt. 24:29).[58] According to St. Peter, the cosmic renewal will be effected through the cleansing of heaven and earth: "But the day of the Lord will come as a thief in the night; in which the heavens shall pass away with a great noise, and the elements shall melt with fervent heat, the earth also and the works that are therein shall be burned up" (2 Pet. 3:10).[59] The things will be consumed, however, "only in order to receive a new quality, while their substance remains the same."[60]

The cataclysmic change, however, will not annihilate the present world; rather it will restore it. The Bible does not use the Greek word neos, meaning new in time or origin, but kainos, meaning new in nature or in quality.[61] So a new heaven and a new earth does not suggest a universe totally other than the present world. Rather, it implies a creation of a universe; though it has been gloriously renewed, the new world stands in continuity with the present world.[62] The judgment, the perspective of continuity and restoration are not mutually exclusive in the Biblical eschatology.[63]

There is no antithesis between the present world and the renewed or new world (palingenesia). Rather, the old world will be renewed to a new one. God will not destroy the works of His hands, but will cleanse them from sin and perfect them, so that they may finally reach the goal for which He created them. He in creation promised that He will make the earth itself His habitation. Accordingly, Adam was placed in the Garden of Eden to rule over the earth. When man sined, his dominion over the earth was not taken away, but the earth over which he ruled was now under a curse (Gen. 3:17) Since the time of the Fall, being so corrupted by sin, man

could no longer execute his creation mandate.
But when Christ comes again, through the two
eschatological processes of resurrection and
judgment, the old world will be cleansed and
renewed to a new heaven and a new earth, and
those in Christ will resume the creation
mandate in their proper performance.

The new world (palingenesia), being a
renewal of the old world, also will have a
cultural continuity with our present culture.
This was implied in St. Paul's teaching that
a person may build on the foundation of faith
in Christ with lasting materials like gold,
silver, or precious stones, so that in the
new world his work may survive and he may
receive a reward (1 Cor. 3:10-15). St. John
also spoke of the deeds which shall follow
those who have died in the Lord (Rev. 14:13).
The cultural continuity between now and then
is also suggested in the fact that the kings
and nations of the earth shall bring their
glory into the new Jerusalem (Rev. 21:24,
26). Although the continuity between now and
then exists, the glory of the new world will
far outshine the glory of the present world
(1 Cor. 2:9).

The redeemed existence in the new world
also will differ from the present order to
such a degree that sex will no longer function as it now does, but that "the sons of
that age" will be like the angels, having no
need for the procreation (Mark 12:25; Lk.
20:35). In the new world, there will be no
more weeping and distress, and no more death
and mourning. The new world will be a realm
of peace and harmony, and a perspective of
righteousness. This great blessing will
extend even to the animal kingdom, and the
wolf and the lamb will feed together (Isa.
65:17-25). God's dwelling place in the new
world will be on the earth, no longer far
away, and nations shall live together in
peace, serving Him (Rev. 22:2),

Then the Judeo-Christian historic-linear eschatology does not teach us that we spend eternity some where off in space. On the contrary, it assures us that on the new earth we shall live to God's praise in glorified, resurrected bodies. On that new earth, Christians will spend eternity, enjoying its beauties, exploring its resources, and using its treasures to the glory of God. This is the third phase of the reigning with Christ.[64]

This shall be the consummation of the Judeo-Christian hope and the ultimate goal of the redemption. Toward this ultimate end the present world moves on. At the end of the course of the present age, the eternal "rest" awaits the people of God. Therefore St. Paul admonishes: "And to you who are troubled rest with us, when the Lord Jesus shall be revealed from heaven with his mighty angels" (2 Th. 1:7).

Notes

Chapter V

1. For the detailed account see Boettnes,
   op. cit., Robert G. Clouse (ed.), The
   Meaning of the Millennium (Downess Grove:
   Inter Varsity Press, 1977), F.E.
   Hamilton, The Basis of MIllennial Faith
   (Grand Rapids: Wm. B. Eerdmans, 1942),
   D.H. Kromminga, The Millennium in the
   Church (Grand Rapids: Wm. B. Eerdmans,
   1945), G.E. Ladd, The Blessed Hope (Grand
   Rapids: Wm. B. Eerdmans, 1956), Hoekema,
   op. cit., G.L. Murray, Millennial Studies
   (Grand Rapids: Baker, 1948).

2. We first met chiliasm in the book of
   Enoch 91 and 93, in the "vision of
   weeks," so called, because it divided the
   entire course of the world duration into
   ten weeks. The eighth of these stands
   for the messianic period, the ninth and
   the tenth bring the final judgment, and
   it is not until the close of the tenth
   week that the new creation appeared. In
   the Sibyline Oracles 652-660, the
   messianic kingdom is represented as being
   destroyed by the assembled nations, and
   after in turn these are destroyed, and
   the kingdom of God begins. Psalm of
   Solomon 17 and 18 describes the messianic
   kingdom as something transitory. In 4
   Ezra 7:28, the messianic kingdom lasts
   for 400 years and then Christ, together
   with all other earthly creatures, dies,
   after which the dead awakes and the eternal judgment occurs. In 4 Ezra 12:34,
   the messianic era lasts till the end of
   the present world and judgment.

3. Cf. Isa. 2:2-4; 40:5; 49:6; 60:1-22; Ezek. 20:34-38; 40-48; Zech. 9:10; Micah 4:7; Hamilton, op, cit., pp. 50 ff.

4. Boettner, op. cit., pp. 55-56.

5. In the book of Revelation, the Church was symbolized by the seven golden candlesticks, the Holy Spirit by seven spirits, and the fulness of the power of Christ by the Lamb having seven horns. The number twelve is the number of the Church, and this number and its multiple are symbolically used: twelve apostles, 24 elders, or the number 144.000 for the totality of His people. The new Jerusalem was pictured as a city in the form of a cube, 12.000 furlongs, a figure which symbolizes perfect grandure and vastness. These are some of many symbols. For further information, see Boettner, op. cit., pp. 63 ff.

6. Refer to note 3.

7. Boettner, op. cit., p. 25.

8. Ibid., p. 26.

9. Zondervan Pictorial Encyclopedia of the Bible, IV, 823. Cf. Matt. 13:33; Rom. 11; Rev. 11:15.

10. Clouse, op. cit., p. 118.

11. E. g. Albertus Pieters, Studies on the Revelation of St. John, p. 305.

12. Ladd, Revelation, pp. 262-263.

13. Ibid., p. 262.

14. E.g. J. F. Walvoord, The Revelation of Jesus Christ (Chicago: Moody Press, 1975), pp. 291-292.

15. Hamilton, op. cit., pp. 132-133.

16. Murray, op. cit., p. 176.

17. P. Gaechter, "The Original Sequence of Apocalypse 20-22," Theological Studies 10(1949), 488-489.

18. Boettner, op. cit., p. 126.

19. Leon Morris, The Revelation of St. John (Grand Rapids: Wm. B. Eerdmans, 1976), p. 126.

20. B.B. Warfield, The Millennium and Apocalypse, in Biblical Doctrine, pp. 649-651.

21. Eanest De Witt Burton, Syntax of the Mood and Tenses in New Testament Greek (Edinburgh: T. and T. Clark, 1955), 31-33.

22. C. Hong, To Whom the Land of Palestine Belongs (Hicksville: Exposition Press, 1979), p. 42.

23. St. Augustine, in line of the significance of the Israelites' status of being "the kingdom of priests," commented the reigning with Christ as referring to: 1. the ruling of the office- bearers over the Church in this presnet life; 2. the subjugation of warring lust by believers in this life; and 3. the reigning of deceased believers with Christ in heaven (the City of God, XX, 9-10).

24. Marselink, op. cit., pp. 206-207.

25. Morris, op. cit., p. 234.

26. Cullmann, op. cit., pp. 194 ff.

27. John Murray, Redemption Accomplished and Applied (Grand Rapids: Wm. B. Eerdmans, 1955), pp. 26-29.

28. E. g. Gal. 3:29; 4:7; Col. 1:12-13; for further information see Hong, op. cit., pp. 80 ff.

29. Ladd prefers the translation, "they came to life again," Revelation, p. 265.

30. Henry Alford, The Greek New Testament, IV, 732-33.

31. Ladd, op. cit., p. 266.

32. Zao, anistemi, egeiro, and anazao.

33. James Hughes, "The Question of the Millenium," Westminster Theological Journal 35 (1973), p. 302.

34. In this regard see Kleine's article, "The First Resurrection," Westminster Theological Journal 27 (Spring, 1975), 366-375. His thesis was developed on the antithetical pairing of "first" and "second" and "old" and "new." He convincingly argued for the metaphorical meaning of "the first resurrection" against the Premillennial literal intereration. Cf. Hamilton, op. cit., p. 123, Boettner, op. cit., p. 264.

35. Hoekema, op. cit., p. 230.

36. Ibid., pp. 229-233; Hamilton, op. cit., pp. 119-120.

37. E. G. Ladd, Clouse (ed.), op. cit., p. 190.

38. Josephus, Ant. XVIII, 1, 4; Wars, II, 8, 14.

39. N. Shepherd, "Postmillennialism" in the Zondervan Pictorical Encyclopedia of the Bible, ed., M.C. Tenney, 1975, IV, 822-23; "The Resurrection of Rev. 20," Westminster Theological Journal XXXVII, I (Fall, 1974), 34-43.

40. See Mark 12:26-27; Jn. 5:24-29; 11:24-26; Rom. 4:13; Eph. 2:4-5; 5:14; Col. 3:1; 2 Tim. 2:11-12; 1 Pet. 3:18.

41. Ladd, Revelation, p. 267.

42. M.C. Tenney, "The Importance and Exegesis of Revelation 20: 1-8," Bibliotheca Sacra III (1954), 137-148.

43. The word "end" is a perfectly definite
one with a set and distinct meaning, cf.
Matt. 24:6, 14; 1 Cor. 1:8; 2 Cor. 1:13,
14. This word is the standing designation of the "end of the ages" or the "end
of the world," Warfield, Biblical and
Theological Studies, p. 484; Hamiltion,
op. cit., pp. 95-96.

44. Berkouwer, op. cit., p. 61.

45. In the Old Testament, Sheoul in general
meant the realm of the dead for both
godly and ungodly, and "grave" (Gen.
37:35; 42:38; 1 Sam. 2:6; Job. 17:13-16;
Prov. 22:20; 30:15-16; Isa. 5:14; Hab.
2:5). However, the conviction that the
lot of the wicked and that of the godly
after death is not the same is gradually
revealed (Ps. 49:14-15; 16:10; cf. Gen.
5:24; 23:10; Acts 2:27, 31).

46. C. Hong, Israel in Ancient Near Eastern
Setting (Ann Arbor: University Microfilms
International, 1980), pp. 29 ff.

47. G. C. Berkouwer, Man, the Image of God
(Grand Rapids: Wm. B. Eerdmans, 1962) pp.
194-233.

48. D. E. H. Whiteley, The Theology of St.
Paul (Philadelphia: Fortress Press,
1066), p. 252.

49. Hoekema, op. cit., p. 252.

50. Vos, op. cit., p. 167; J. H. Shep, The
Nature of the Resurrection Body (Grand
Rapids: Wm. B. Eerdmans, 1964), ch. 6.

51. Rom. 2:5; 3:6; 13:2; 1 Cor. 4:5; 11:32; 2
Th. 2:12; 2 Tim. 4:1.

52. The one who sat on the throne is God the Father (Rev. 5:1, 7, 13; 20:12). Sometimes the Scripture says that Christ is to be the judge of all (Matt. 25;31 ff.; Jn. 5:22). St. Paul refers both to the judgment seat of Christ (2 Cor. 5:10), and to that of God (Rom. 14:10). Morris, op. cit., p. 241.

53. Matt. 16:27; 25:31-46; Rev. 20:11-13. Premillennialism suggests that nations and individuals will be judged in relation to their attitude toward the Jews. It appeals for support to Matt. 25:40, where Christ said "my brethren." On other occasions, Christ called unbelieving Jews "children of the devil and synagogue of Satan" (Rev. 2:9; 3:9).

54. Matt. 6:4, 6, 18; 12:36; 25:35-40; Lk. 12:2; Rom. 2:16; 1 Cor. 3:8; 4:5; Eph. 6:8; 1 Tim. 5:24-25; Heb. 6:10; 1 Pet. 1:17; Rev. 20:12; 22:12.

55. Hoekema, op. cit., p. 261.

56. Ibid., p. 254.

57. Ant. 11:3-9. Philo also used it for the renewal of the world after the flood, Vita Mos. 11, 12, and for the restoration of the world after being burned, de Mund, XV.

58. Cf. Isa. 13:10; 34:4; Ezek 32:7; Joel 2:10, 31; 3:15; Hag. 2:6, 21; Rev. 6:12, 13.

59. Cf. Ps. 102:25-26; Acts 3:21; 1 Cor. 7:31.

60. Calvin on 2 Pet. 3:10.

61. TDNT III, 447-449.

62. Hoekema, op. cit., pp. 280-281.

63. Berkouwer, op. cit., p. 203. This also was the late Jewish idea, 1 En. 45:4-5; 48:7; 61:15; 2 Esdras 7:75; 2 Bar. 32:6, and so on.

64. Hoekema, op. cit., p. 274; Rev. 19:1-8; 22:3.

INDEX

174

Lincoln Christian College

DATE DUE

DEC 8 '82			
Reserve Summer '87			
F			

DEMCO 38-297